LITIGATION TO LIFE

LITIGATION TO LIFE

AN INJURY VICTIM'S GUIDE TO NAVIGATING THE SETTLEMENT PROCESS

JASON D. LAZARUS

HOUNDSTOOTH
PRESS

LITIGATION TO LIFE
An Injury Victim's Guide to Navigating the Settlement Process

FIRST EDITION

ISBN   978-1-5445-4186-0 *Hardcover*
        978-1-5445-4187-7 *Paperback*
        978-1-5445-4188-4 *Ebook*

For over twenty years, I have had the opportunity and privilege to work with people experiencing some of the most difficult and possibly worst periods in their lives. These clients have entrusted me to counsel them regarding important issues they face when resolving their cases. The people I have worked with, their families, and their stories have inspired me. I have dedicated my career to helping improve their lives, but my life also has been touched immensely by all those I have worked with. This book is dedicated to all of them: the survivors!

CONTENTS

What makes my extensive legal experience even more relevant is that, like you, I have suffered a personal injury and have been through the entire personal injury lawsuit process myself. I can tell you without a doubt, it was one of the most difficult things I have been through thus far in my life. Even though I had helped thousands of accident victims plan for their own settlements, even though I was an attorney who knew the issues inside out, and even though I had a trusted friend and colleague representing me in my personal injury case, none of that prepared me for what I experienced after I was hit by a car while cycling.

INTRODUCTION

When I get out on my bike early in the morning as the sun is rising, I feel this sense of amazement that I can't explain. I raced competitively in my early to late teenage years, kept cycling to keep fit, and started racing again in my forties. I remember feeling strong and fast on that summer morning in August 2016 when I rolled out alone to meet up with my favorite cycling group. I had been training hard and was probably in the best shape I had been in since I was a teenager. That day, I turned out of my neighborhood and onto a two-lane road with a bike lane, as was my usual routine. I had the right of way as I rode northbound in the bike lane. While riding, I saw headlights coming toward me

from the opposite direction. Just as I reached a small shopping plaza on my right, the truck, whose headlights I had seen, suddenly turned into the plaza's parking lot and struck me.

I don't remember being hit. I just remember the headlights glaring into my eyes, my internal voice screaming, "NO!" and then the faint memory of lying on the ground while a bystander came to my aid. He turned me on my side so the blood could flow out of my bleeding face. The next thing I remember was briefly waking 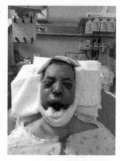 up in the emergency room of my local level-one trauma center. I later learned that I had surgery that same evening and was heavily sedated. After a medically induced five-day coma, I finally regained full consciousness, awakening to find that my jaw was wired shut and I was on a ventilator. I could not verbally communicate since I had two tubes stuck down my throat, one to breathe and a feeding tube to keep me nourished. I knew I was pretty banged up but had no idea of the extent of my injuries. I would later learn that all the bones in my face were broken—literally. I was diagnosed with a LeFort III fracture, meaning all facial bones are broken, including the eye orbits and nose. My jaw had been broken in multiple places, and I needed a metal plate in my chin to fix a midline fracture. The impact ripped my lower lip in half and knocked out seven of my upper teeth; it also broke my right collarbone, requiring a plate and screws. After being on the ventilator for a week or so in the ICU, I had so much pain in my broken jaw that the doctors had to instead insert the breathing tube directly into my windpipe through an incision in the front of my neck, known as a tracheotomy.

It took me three weeks to get off the ventilator, allowing me to once again breathe on my own and to be able to swallow liquids without a feeding tube. It took two more months to be able to eat solid food and two years of extensive dental work before I could eat normally again.

As a result of being struck while cycling, I lost a lot of time that I won't ever get back. I couldn't work for two months as talking and nutrition was very difficult with my jaw wired shut. I still can't enjoy food the way I used to since I constantly bite my lips and the insides of my cheeks when I eat. Because of my dental injuries and jaw injuries, I still have jaw pain, my mouth doesn't open or close the same as it used to, food gets caught in my dental implants, and my mouth always feels abnormal. Our board of directors had to temporarily take over my responsibilities as CEO of Synergy, and of course I could not help grow the business further by speaking publicly or writing articles. Cycling, a sport and hobby I love, and exercise that is an investment in my own wellness, was nearly taken away from me. I was able to get back on the bike eventually, but cycling will never, ever be the same because of my fear of being hit again; when I cycle, I'm in a state of constant paranoia about the cars that are close to me on the road.

While the physical damage to my body from the collision was significant, the emotional and psychological damages were equally so. The indignities and complete loss of control I suffered in the hospital caused scars that cannot be reversed. I suffered significant post-traumatic stress symptoms and sought counseling. My family was terrified—especially my children—to see me in such a vulnerable condition as they wondered whether I was going to survive. And as if that trauma wasn't bad enough, I also experienced the intense stress of suddenly having to figure out insurance, manage health care expenditures in the six figures, file a lawsuit, and determine what kind of settlement would allow me to resume my life and protect my financial future.

When I settled my case, after a year and a half of litigation, in the back of my mind I knew my medical insurance plan had a lien against my settlement. I knew I was getting a large sum of money that I needed to manage. I knew I was going to have future medical expenses that couldn't exactly be quantified, and I didn't know when I would incur those expenses. So, I had to take on those issues myself (since that is what I do for a living). You may ask yourself, what did he do? Well, I did what I talk about throughout this book. I thought about what I wanted my future to look like as I transitioned from litigation to life. Once I thought through it all, I developed a plan; that meant I fought the lien holder to reduce the lien. I evaluated things like structured settlements and trusts to protect the recovery. Then, once I finalized the net proceeds, I decided upon a plan after negotiating the lien.

For the most part, my experiences will be like yours at settlement. You probably will feel overwhelmed, anxious, and uncertain. That is when you should rely upon those around you whom you trust. Your personal injury attorney has been through this before and can be an invaluable resource and guide. Typically, you will have other professionals to help you with some of the more complicated issues I address in this book. Having a team of experts to help you with what quite possibly may be some of the most important decisions in your life is critical to ensuring you have the best possible outcome.

Coincidentally, I had built a business based on doing just that for other people—but my life's work took on new meaning after I experienced being a victim firsthand and making that transition from litigation to life myself.

* * *

I share my experience to illustrate that I have intimate knowledge of what it's like to be in your shoes, to have your whole life changed, maybe permanently, in one terrifying moment. In an instant, things are turned upside down. You can no longer care for yourself. People who depend on you can no longer do so. You might miss work or never work again or be stuck paying off medical bills, all while trying to still take care of your family. Your injuries might linger for the rest of your life, and the recovery, rehabilitation, and medical expenses from your injuries can be a massive burden on you and your family—especially if you can no longer work.

Maybe you are one of the 3 million people injured in car accidents every year in the United States (according to the National Highway Traffic Safety Administration) or one of the 4.5 million people injured on the job (according to the National Safety Council) or a relative of one of the approximately 250,000 annual fatalities from medical malpractice (according to a John Hopkins Medicine study). These accidents/adverse incidents contribute to the 300,000 to 500,000 annual personal injury lawsuits, with only 5 percent of those cases making it into a courtroom, according to US government statistics.

As if the trauma of being injured by someone else isn't enough on its own, you also have to contend with the difficult litigation that results when you file a personal injury lawsuit to recover damages for your injuries. While the lawsuit can help secure your financial stability and ensure your future medical needs are met, it also plunges you into daunting litigation that almost always resolves before trial, leaving you with a lot of high-stakes questions to answer about your future, and often in a very short period of time.

While I cannot take away the pain you continue to suffer or the emotional impact of your injuries, I can help unravel this intimidating plethora of legalities, provide information that will give you the best shot of creating a sound plan for your settlement, and, most importantly, get you back to living your life.

You will learn:

- **Why taking the entire settlement as one lump sum might seem like a good idea, but in most cases, is not;**
- **How to protect your eligibility for government health care**

plans if your settlement cannot pay for all of your future needs;

- How, once your settlement is finalized, health insurance companies come after you with reimbursement claims that are, sadly, legitimate, and how you can deal with them;
- How the most important financial decision of your life requires a team of experts working to protect your best interests; and
- How anticipating these decisions as early as possible in your case is one of the best things you can do to maximize your settlement and protect your recovery.

Being an accident victim is emotionally draining; you did nothing wrong, but someone has harmed you. It is also physically draining. Add on the stress of litigation, and by the time you get to settlement, you are at the end of what will have been a very difficult period in your life. The decisions you must make as part of the settlement process are extremely important and cannot be overlooked. The long-term impact of making the wrong choice can be devastating. While no amount of money is enough to compensate you or your family for what you went through, it will help. But the reality is that there are only so many dollars available, and the insurance company/defendant is willing to pay you only so much to settle your case.

For decades, I have been helping unravel these issues at settlement on behalf of victims like you. As a young defense attorney, I hated working on behalf of the people who caused the injuries (the defense side), as I never felt like I did any good or helped anyone. I decided to switch careers and put my legal training to work in the area of settlement consulting—assisting trial lawyers and injury victims as they settle catastrophic cases. By working for injury victims (the plaintiff side), I was able to create sound settlement plans and see the immense difference they made for the impacted people and their families. It was a rewarding way to help people in their most vulnerable state.

It all seemed simple enough when I started my settlement planning practice, but as the years went by, I started to understand how truly complex the settlement planning and settlement process is. I realized that not enough experts really understand the intersection of taxes, damages, government compliance, and so forth; and as a result, too many injured victims are under-advised about these important issues. Trying to make complex issues easily understandable for injury victims became my professional goal.

In 2008, I started my own company, Synergy Settlement Services, with a mission to improve the lives of the catastrophically injured. Synergy now serves thousands of injury victims each year. Day in and day out, we help injury victims transition from litigation to life by dealing with all of the issues that arise during the settlement process. We work closely with personal injury attorneys across the country to make sure they maximize their clients' recoveries and implement the best possible settlement plans for their clients. Like most settlement experts, my team members get paid as experts at the conclusion of personal injury cases. There are usually no upfront fees for these types of services other than small administrative fees typically paid at intake. For lien resolution services, fees are based on a percentage of savings. Medicare compliance work is flat-fee-based. Settlement planning services—preparing plans and putting together teams of experts to serve clients as they transition from settlement to life afterward—are commission and/or consulting-fee-based.

This book presents an overview of the most pressing legal issues at settlement so that you can understand all the considerations that go into a personal injury settlement and make sure that you and your team are addressing all of them. However, this book is not intended to be legal advice. You should always rely upon your lawyer and his or her law firm to advise you about the legal issues involved in your case. Similarly, issues around preserving government benefits can vary from state to state, so having a local elder law attorney assist you at settlement is always best. I also recommend, in "complex" cases, that your legal team include a tax attorney, as well as a competent CPA or other tax planning expert.

Of course, I would have preferred not to have been injured due to someone else's negligence, and I am sure that you share this sentiment. But I also am grateful—grateful for the incredible doctors, nurses, and other medical professionals who helped me recover and for the legal system that gave me the opportunity to have my damages addressed and to face the person who forever changed my life with his negligence. I am also grateful to you for allowing me to steer you through this tumultuous time, from litigation to life.

A WORD ABOUT HOW TO USE THIS BOOK

This book is my second. My first book, *Art of Settlement*, was a guide for trial lawyers navigating the complex issues which can arise at settlement. This second book is written for you, the injury victim, to help guide you through the decision-making process that is part of settling/resolving a personal injury case. In the chapters that follow, you will find guidance on issues ranging from the basics of the settlement process to the complexities of managing the recovery along with government benefit preservation and ending with resolution of liens. Some chapters have a related appendix which I suggest you read with that particular chapter to get the best educational experience.

CHAPTER 1

YOU HAVE BEEN INJURED. WHAT'S NEXT?

I had been assisting personal injury lawyers and their clients at settlement for seventeen years when I was struck by that truck while cycling, so I was one of the few victims who knew exactly what I needed to do next. Given all that I suffered from being struck while cycling, I hired a personal injury attorney, who happened to be a friend. When he visited me in the hospital, I still couldn't speak, and so I wrote notes to him with a pen and paper. We soon learned that when the driver hit me, he was turning into the parking lot to go to the bagel shop where he worked. He had the minimum coverage in our home state of Florida, a $10,000 policy. Unfortunately, this is very common where there is insufficient (or even zero) insurance coverage on the part of the defendant. Thankfully, I had purchased quite a bit of underinsured motorist (UM/UIM) coverage through my own personal auto insurance policy, which should have covered me. However, my insurance company refused to pay, even though the liability was clear. Thus, I joined most injury victims who must sue their own insurance company. I was deposed twice, and the case eventually went to mediation, where I got the opportunity to look the driver in the eye and explain the tremendous impact that his negligence had on my life, my family, and my business. My case ultimately settled at mediation after two years of litigation.

While the settlement brought me great relief and catharsis, it necessitated decisions about how to protect my recovery and how the settlement should be structured. I had anticipated these decisions and ultimately made choices that I had spent years recommending to my own clients. But the vast majority of victims have, of course, never anticipated being involved in a personal injury case and are not nearly as equipped to make these decisions so quickly.

In this chapter, I lay out the major decisions and steps that you can anticipate in the settlement process. My goal is for you to have the space to make these decisions well in advance so that when the time comes for settlement negotiations, you are ready.

SELECTING AN ATTORNEY

When a person is injured in an accident, and the accident is the fault of a third party, the third party's insurance is responsible for compensating the victim...in theory. While in certain cases insurance companies do pay injury victims, such cases are rare. More commonly, the third party's insurance company refuses to pay for the damages the victim has suffered. At that point, if they haven't already, most victims turn to a personal injury attorney who can file claims against the insurance company (or companies) to get the compensation the victim deserves.

If you are reading this book, you have likely already hired a personal injury attorney, but if not, consider these things when looking for a lawyer to represent you. Hiring the right personal injury attorney can mean the difference between being made whole and suffering under the massive weight of disability and debt. First and foremost, you want someone you can trust and who has taken the time to understand your injuries and your case. Hiring an attorney who specializes in personal injury law is important, as well as someone who is both a talented litigator and a skilled negotiator. He or she must also be adept at investigating the firms of potential attorneys in terms of age, size, experience, and amount of resources available to handle your case. As part of your due diligence, find out what past clients say about the lawyers and firms you are considering.

As you interview attorneys, ask these questions:

- Have you tried this type of personal injury case before?
- What types of verdicts have you obtained in these types of cases?
- Do you have the time necessary to work on my case right now?
- If not you, who will be responsible for my case?
- How will you let me know what is happening in my case?
- Do you think we will need to go to trial?
- What is your comfort level regarding going to trial?
- What are examples of past settlements you have negotiated?
- What types of experts will be assisting you with my case to address issues such as liens, government benefits, tax issues, and financial planning issues?
- Who are they and how will they be compensated?
- What are your contingency fee and costs? Will I be responsible for any advanced costs if we lose?

- What do you believe is the likely outcome of my case?

YOU HIRED AN ATTORNEY – NOW, THE ROAD TO SETTLEMENT

Most of the time, your attorney will wind up filing a lawsuit against the liable third party and his or her insurance company (assuming there is insurance coverage) to state a claim for the damages you have suffered. However, before filing suit, your lawyer's first move most likely will be to make a demand for payment from the liable third party's insurance company. This gives the insurance company an opportunity to pay you without the need to file a lawsuit. The demand will outline the damages you have suffered, including the damages a plaintiff in a personal injury case typically claims: economic damages, such as past and future medical expenses and lost wages, as well as non-economic damages, such as pain and suffering, mental anguish, and loss of companionship. These non-economic damages are the physical and/or emotional pain and suffering you endured because of someone else's negligence. Sometimes, there are also claims asserted for "punitive" damages to punish a wrongdoer (although that is rarer). Insurance companies generally refuse the initial demand for payment which typically leads to a lawsuit being filed.

As I mentioned in the introduction, the vast majority of personal injury cases—95 percent—result in an out-of-court settlement. The timing of these settlements varies widely. The settlement might come before any formal legal action is taken, right after a lawsuit is filed, or at mediation after months or even years of litigation. It could also be on the courthouse steps, right before a trial is set to begin. Most cases end up at least proceeding through the discovery process, which involves the exchange of information between the legal teams as well as the interrogatories and depositions of the victim and other people in the case. Some cases require a judge's involvement to make rulings on various legal issues that will push the case toward a resolution. Most cases, like mine, go to mediation, which is a settlement conference attended by the parties and a neutral third-party mediator who is often an experienced attorney or retired judge.

When a case settles at mediation, the terms of that agreement are documented in the mediation agreement and then ultimately memorialized in a settlement agreement or release. If the case is not resolved at mediation, typically the lawyers for each side continue to negotiate by exchanging a series of demands or offers to settle, usually ending in a settlement agreement or release. The settlement agreement/release can have a profound impact on your future and the kind of care that may be available to you to treat your injuries, as well as the amount of money accessible to you. Understanding and thinking through the issues, with your team of experts, well in advance of the actual settlement is best, as the timing of settlements can be unpredictable, and you must make most of the decisions quickly or you could face a delay in receiving the settlement money. Most major settlement decisions fall into one of three categories:

CATEGORY #1: HOW TO MANAGE THE FINANCIAL PROCEEDS

How and when should you receive the money from the settlement? As noted before, receiving it all in a lump sum does not work out well for the vast majority of victims. So, should you ask for a structured settlement? Should you utilize a trust? Are there any public benefit preservation issues that will determine what type of trust needs to be created? What are the tax implications of all these choices? What special language needs to be in the settlement agreement or release if exercising specific options for managing the financial recovery? Chapter 3 explores these questions in more depth.

CATEGORY #2: WHO WILL PROVIDE FUTURE HEALTH CARE COVERAGE?

Of course, you want to make sure that you have adequate health care to properly recover from the injuries you have suffered. But how you obtain that health care is quite complicated and requires planning and analysis. Some of the questions that should be answered are:

- Given your circumstances, should public benefits such as Medicaid be kept in place, or would it be better for you to obtain private coverage?
- Will future Medicare eligibility be jeopardized?

Chapters 4, 5, and 6 explore this highly complex set of issues. Then, Chapter 7 shows how all of this information can be used to craft an effective settlement plan.

CATEGORY #3: NEGOTIATING AND RESOLVING HEALTH CARE LIENS

As if the first two categories of decisions weren't enough to think about, most likely, you also will get hit by liens at settlement: bills that your health insurance company paid on your behalf and are owed back after you get money for your injuries. Chapter 8 is a deep dive into this subject.

The remaining chapters of this book educate you about these three categories of decisions you face at settlement in order to make an informed choice as to what is right for you and your family. I will help you navigate these decisions that will enable you to successfully transition from litigation to life.

What makes my extensive legal experience even more relevant is that, like you, I have suffered a personal injury and have been through the entire personal injury lawsuit process myself. I can tell you without a doubt, it was one of the most difficult things I have been through thus far in my life. Even though I had helped thousands of accident victims plan for their own settlements, even though I was an attorney who knew the issues inside out, and even though I had a trusted friend and colleague representing me in my personal injury case, none of that prepared me for what I experienced after I was hit by a car while cycling.

Chapter 2

THE IMPORTANCE OF PLANNING FOR YOUR SETTLEMENT

WHY DO YOU NEED A PLAN FOR YOUR SETTLEMENT?

A recent study conducted by The National Leadership Consortium on Developmental Disabilities entitled "Future Financial Planning for People with Disabilities: What's Working and What's Not" identified certain potential reasons that those who are disabled fail to plan. Among the top reasons for failing to set up a plan, listed by the disabled and their families, are: 1) not enough money to do it; 2) too expensive; 3) afraid to lose benefits; 4) afraid rules will change; 5) don't know enough about them; and 6) worried money won't be safe (though it most likely will be safe if they work with a team of settlement experts). The study also identified some of the top legal and societal barriers that people with disabilities face in terms of the planning process: 1) people with disabilities do not get the help they need to plan and save their money; 2) many in society believe that people with disabilities cannot understand, manage, and save money; and 3) rules and laws are too complicated for people with disabilities to use effectively. Because of the foregoing misconceptions, as well as others, oftentimes injury victims fail to plan at all at settlement. This results in settlements being paid out entirely in lump-sum fashion, which can have serious, negative, long-term impacts on someone who is seriously injured and disabled.

Taking your entire settlement in one lump sum without a specific plan often sounds like a good idea to injury victims. After all, the money is immediately available to you whenever you need or want it. So, it may come as a shock to learn that anecdotal evidence suggests that most American personal injury victims dissipate their settlements very rapidly. This phenomenon is likely connected to "sudden wealth syndrome," a term used to describe the issues experienced by people who suddenly receive a large sum of money, including adjustment, stress, confusion, and often mismanagement. For example, many professional athletes go bankrupt after retiring. According to a 2009 report by *Sports Illustrated*, 78 percent of NFL players have gone bankrupt or are under financial stress within two years of retirement, and an estimated 60 percent of all former NBA players are broke.

The reasons for loss of sudden wealth can be manyfold. First on the list is out-of-control spending. Second is making unwise investment decisions with the money. Third is trusting the wrong people to assist you. Fourth is using money to help other family members instead of protecting it for your own future needs. All of this means that of all the hundreds of thousands of personal injury victims in the United States each year, you must be in the top tier of money managers to have *anything* left of your settlement three to five years after you receive it.

Choosing a financial settlement option that is not appropriate for your situation can have devastating consequences. Health care options can be compromised, and money that is meant to last a lifetime can instead dissipate quickly.

To avoid making mistakes that could be very costly for your financial future post-settlement, consider a few strategies to employ. First, educate yourself on your financial options at settlement. This portion of the book will help you do just that! But also, after settling your case, figure out what you need to do to live comfortably from a financial perspective. From there, a team of experts, including a qualified settlement planner, can help you create a sound, comprehensive financial settlement plan for the money you receive that will meet your needs. Thereafter, you need to maintain discipline: stay with your chosen plan and use a budget to keep spending in check. You also need a team of trusted professionals who can assist you post-settlement, including financial, tax, and legal professionals. Lastly, avoid doing anything you do not understand in terms of the financial settlement plan.

WHY DO YOU NEED A SETTLEMENT PLANNER?

The topics in the remainder of this book can seem foreign or overly complex, even for many lawyers whose practices are dedicated to representing injury victims. That is because personal injury settlement consulting is a highly specialized area that combines complex legal, disability, and financial issues. As a settlement expert, I have dedicated my career to working through these issues and helping victims understand them.

A settlement is meant to last the remainder of your life, and therefore it probably will be the most important financial transaction of your life. No two settlements are the same, and the process is complex. As you go through the process of resolving your case, relying on an experienced and highly credentialed expert who understands all of the issues, explores all of the options, and provides customized settlement planning advice is vitally important. This expert can also ensure that you are properly protected in any transaction involving the defendant's insurance company and a structured settlement. For those who are disabled and have special needs that require a lifetime of financial support, this expert is particularly crucial. A settlement planner understands the myriad of wealth management issues and knows how to use public benefit preservation techniques to ensure that you are taken care of financially and that you do not lose public benefits when the settlement proceeds are disbursed. What's more, settlement planning experts understand that victims who have lost their ability to earn cannot take the same investment risks as people who can absorb losses in the market by replacing losses with future earnings.

A settlement planner should meet with you to identify your financial needs as well as any public benefit programs that need to be kept in place. Using this information, he or she should design a customized settlement plan for your recovery, utilizing the right combination of traditional financial products and legal documents, including professionally managed accounts, trusts, and structured settlements. A properly devised plan provides you with liquidity, lifelong security, and tax-free rates of return, removing the primary concerns post-settlement. A solid settlement plan both maximizes the amount of money you will get from the settlement and protects it for the long term.

Typically, experienced trial lawyers hire settlement planning experts because they recognize the value of this type of service for their injury victim clients. If your lawyer hasn't hired such an expert, then you should request that he or she do so, or you can hire someone yourself in consultation with your lawyer. When choosing a settlement planner, look for someone with one or more of the following professional credentials: a juris doctor (law) degree; financial planning certifications, such as a Certified Structured Settlement Consultant (CSSC), Master's Certificate in Structured Settlement Consulting (MSSC), Registered Settlement Planner (RSP), or a Certified Financial Planner (CFP); Medicare credentials, such as Medicare Set-Aside Consultant Certified (MSCC); and disability planning credentials, such as a Masters of Law in Elder Law (LL.M.) or Chartered Special Needs Consultant (ChSNC).

While your personal injury lawyer is skilled at handling personal injury cases, the issues at settlement are complex and require different knowledge and skills from a litigator. To make sure you are protected and that your settlement is maximized using specialized planning techniques, you need a settlement expert on your team.

CHAPTER 3

SETTLEMENT DECISIONS: FINANCIAL CONSIDERATIONS AND OPTIONS AT SETTLEMENT

This chapter explores the three major options for taking your settlement. First, I go through Option One, a lump sum, examining its positives and its many negatives. I spend the most time on Option Two, a structured settlement, which allows you to receive future periodic payments via a structured settlement annuity and which often is the cornerstone of a comprehensive settlement plan. Finally, I examine Option Three, a settlement trust, established to manage the financial recovery.

It is important to note that these options aren't mutually exclusive, and most victims choose a combination of the three options. When I settled my own personal injury case, I did just that: I received some of the money upfront, some in a structured settlement, and some in a trust. I'll discuss why at the end of this chapter.

OPTION ONE: LUMP SUM

If you exercise this option exclusively, you receive all the personal injury recovery in a single lump-sum payment. This places you in the position of managing a sum of money that might need to last for the rest of your life—for all of your future medical and living expenses. Since most people are not skilled at handling large sums of money, this is a very dangerous option for most injury victims. The previous chapter contains numerous examples of the dangers of sudden wealth.

Another disadvantage of taking a lump-sum payment is that although you do not have to pay taxes on a lump-sum payment for your personal injuries, once you invest the money, you have to pay income taxes on the interest earned. As a rule, taxes continue to go up, not down; so over time, more of your interest will go to the government. There is also a danger that your future needs will not be met because of poor investment returns and the effect of paying taxes on your investments.

What's more, your lump-sum settlement will be exposed to creditor claims, judgments, and division of assets should you get a divorce. And, of course, a lump sum is an easy target for predators in general, which is an especially troubling problem for those with special needs. Here are a few real-life examples of ways people have lost all or part of their lump-sum settlements:

- In 1980, a Tennessee minor's settlement was invested by her father in his construction business. That company failed ten years later, and the entire settlement was lost.
- Between 1997 and 1999, a Florida man's guardian spent the man's 2.2-million-dollar guardianship on frivolous personal items, leaving only $20,000 in the account.

- A 24-year-old cerebral palsy victim from New York with ongoing medical needs lost almost 25 percent of his settlement after his guardian hired an investment firm that made questionable choices in junk bonds and technology stocks, according to *The New York Times*.
- A Florida man, rendered a quadriplegic in an auto accident, received a 2-million-dollar settlement. Unfortunately, the money was stolen by his wife, who used it to pay for her addiction to drugs while ignoring the man's medical needs. He eventually died from neglect and lack of medical treatment.

There's one more major concern, and it's a big one. A lump-sum payment also impacts your ability to receive public assistance, wiping away any needs-based public benefits or reduction in insurance premiums that you might receive through the Affordable Care Act.

Despite all these drawbacks, injury victims typically take a portion of the settlement proceeds as a lump sum so they have money on hand if their circumstances change. I will discuss this further when I address the benefits of trusts.

OPTION TWO: STRUCTURED SETTLEMENTS

The second option for your settlement is receiving periodic payments from a special type of annuity known as a structured settlement. These payments can be monthly, quarterly, semi-annual, or annual. A structured settlement has multiple benefits: its investment gains are never taxed, it offers "spendthrift protection" (protection from spending the settlement money too quickly), and it has enhanced protection against creditor claims as well as judgments. A structured settlement recipient can even avoid disqualification from government assistance when the settlement is used with the appropriate public benefit preservation trust, which I discuss later in this book. However, a structured settlement alone does not protect your needs-based public benefits.

The downside of a structured settlement is that once it is set up, the terms cannot be changed. It is not liquid or flexible like a lump sum. You cannot withdraw money or change the payment terms without a "penalty" via factoring (selling) or a commutation (lump sum payout at death). This is why a structured settlement often is used for only part of the money received from a settlement.

HOW STRUCTURED SETTLEMENTS WORK

The federal government created tax breaks and protections for structured settlement annuities because of all the disadvantages and risks associated with taking an entire personal injury recovery in the form of a lump sum. A structured settlement is a federally income tax-free annuity only available to personal injury victims. Its major benefits are that it transfers the obligation to pay the settlement to a large, financially secure life insurance company; it is managed without ongoing expenses; and it provides an income stream for the rest of your life (or for a guaranteed period of time that can be paid to your beneficiary if you die before that time). Over half a million injury victims receive benefits from structured settlement annuities. Each year, life insurance companies receive billions of settlement monies to fund new structured settlement arrangements, and an estimated $184 billion has been paid in total to fund structured settlements in force since the seventies.[1] Since 1976, more than 998,000 cases have been settled using a structured settlement for all or part of the settlement.[2]

Structured settlements are used in the resolution of so many cases because they offer tax-free income payments, fixed low-risk competitive returns (there are also indexed as well as variable products offered), guaranteed lifetime income, no-cost financial management, spendthrift protection, creditor protection, and avoidance of guardianship requirements in certain cases.[3] Structured settlements offer injury victims the ability to make one-time simple investment decisions that provide competitive returns with no market risk and no income taxation. Similarly, injury victims can also use the annuity as a funding mechanism for other investments using a dollar-cost-averaging approach.[4] In addition, a structured settlement can be a tool to pass wealth on to the next generation, avoiding income tax on any of the income generated.[5]

---

1   Daniel W. Hindert and Craig H. Ulman, "Transfers of Structured Settlement Payment Rights: What Judges Should Know about Structured Settlement Protection Acts," *The Judges' Journal* 44, no. 2 (Spring 2005): 19–31, https://www.jmwsettlements.com/structured_settlements/Article%20Reprints/JudgesJournalUlmanHindert0605.pdf; Patrick J. Hindert, "Future Financial Planning for People with Disabilities—Part 2," *Independent Life* (blog), November 22, 2021, https://www.independent.life/blog/future-financial-planning-for-people-with-disabilities-part-2-2/.

2   Patrick J. Hindert, "Structured Settlement 2016 Annuity Sales," *Beyond Structured Settlements* (blog), February 23, 2017, https://s2kmblog.typepad.com/rethinking_structured_set/2017/02/structured-settlement-2016-annuity-sales.html.

3   See I.R.C. §104(a) (2008), https://www.irs.gov/pub/irs-drop/rr-04-55.pdf. See also Rev. Rul. 79-220 (July 1979). (Payments are income-tax-free to injury victim and all subsequent payees.) [Jessica: I un-italized "*See*" and "*See also*" per https://www.chicagomanualofstyle.org/book/ed17/part3/ch14/psec042.html]

4   Richard B. Risk, Jr., "Structured Settlements: The Ongoing Evolution from a Liability Insurer's Ploy to an Injury Victim's Boon," *Tulsa Law Journal* 36, no. 4 (Summer 2001): 865–903, https://digitalcommons.law.utulsa.edu/cgi/viewcontent.cgi?article=2331&context=tlr.

5   While structured settlements are income-tax-free, even to subsequent payees, they are not estate-tax-free. The present value of the remaining guaranteed payments is includable in the injury victim's gross estate.

WHAT EXACTLY IS A STRUCTURED SETTLEMENT ANNUITY?

An annuity is a life insurance product designed to turn a lump-sum investment into an income stream. It is typically fixed, meaning the rate of return is not based on the performance of the stock market. It can be variable if desired and appropriately based on risk tolerance and the financial situation. This fictional example illustrates how a fixed annuity works:

> Say that out of a $2 million settlement, your settlement planner recommends putting $1 million into a structured settlement annuity for your future needs. That income stream would provide you $3,000 a month, tax-free. If you died prematurely, the payments could continue for 30 years to your named beneficiary (who would also receive them tax-free). If you live more than 30 years, the annuity payments would continue until your death. Another option would be to set up payments that increase annually by 3 percent to accommodate cost-of-living increases. In this case, your monthly check amount would start out much lower—at about $1,400—but would eventually pay out much more than the level annuity. You could also set up monthly payments for your needs, plus an annual lump sum for unforeseen expenses.

IMPORTANT THINGS TO UNDERSTAND ABOUT STRUCTURED SETTLEMENTS

One of the most important things to know is that you must decide whether to set up a structured settlement *before* the defendant pays out the money. Generally, the defendant must fund the structured settlement annuity directly, without anyone associated with the plaintiff ever touching the funds. The annuity is owned by a subsidiary of the life insurance company called an assignment corporation, but you are the beneficiary (the recipient of the payments); this arrangement allows you to receive the payments tax-free.

A structured settlement is not like a bank account where you can simply withdraw funds. You cannot accelerate, defer, or change the payments you receive after the plan is created. While this is an advantage, as it offers spendthrift protection, it is also a disadvantage. You must give up some element of control over the money in order to get the structured settlement tax break.

When used as the cornerstone of a sound financial settlement plan, a structured settlement is an extremely flexible financial product that can be designed to meet your individual needs. It can be used to fund a life insurance policy to provide for additional care in the event that a family member who is a primary caretaker passes away. In a case where there will most likely be expensive future medical needs, the structured settlement can stretch out the proceeds to make them last a lifetime. The structure's payments can even increase over time to keep up with inflation by using a cost-of-living adjustment feature. A structured settlement provides cost-free financial management for your future. There are no ongoing fees, and the life insurance company is obligated to pay you the benefits you have selected regardless of how the market performs.

Structured settlement annuity contracts are issued by large, well-capitalized life insurance companies, including well-known ones like Berkshire Hathaway, MetLife, New York Life, and Pacific Life. There are also some new entrants into the structured settlement marketplace, like Independent Life, who are creating innovative products for injury victims. Due to their financial strength, life insurance companies, when utilized for a structured settlement annuity, make for a very low-risk investment. Your settlement planning expert should do an analysis of the financial strength of any company that is proposed for a structured settlement. You can also diversify your financial risk by spreading your annuity investments among multiple top-rated companies instead of using only one.

In addition, structured settlements offer enhanced protection under the law in case of divorce or bankruptcy. Because they are not owned by the injury victim, they are not assets that can generally be divided or taken away from the victim in the case of divorce.[6] The income that the settlement produces may be considered in determining alimony, but the asset itself usually is not divided.[7] Depending on state law, a structured settlement annuity may not be an asset reachable in personal bankruptcy, meaning you won't necessarily lose your structured settlement annuity payments in the event you must declare bankruptcy.[8]

Structured settlements are a very important planning tool for injury victims. Because of their security, tax-free returns, and general shield against creditors, they should be considered as part of a comprehensive settlement plan. Because of the

---

6   See generally *Krebs v. Krebs*, 435 N.W.2d 240 (Wis. 1989).

7   See generally *Ihlenfeldt v. Ihlenfeldt*, 549 N.W.2d 791 (Wis. App. 1996).

8   See *In re McCollam*, 612 So.2d 572 (Fla. 1993). Annuity was exempt under Florida Statute 222.14 from creditor claims in bankruptcy action. See also *In re Orso*, 283 F.3d 686 (5th Cir. 2002) (holding structured settlement "annuity contracts under which payments were owed came within scope of Louisiana statute exempting such contracts from the claims of creditors"); *In re Belue*, 238 B.R. 218 (S.D. Fla. 1999) (holding "debtor who was named, as payee and intended beneficiary, under annuity purchased by insurance company to fund its obligations under structured settlement agreement was entitled to claim annuity payments as exempt under special Florida exemption for proceeds of any annuity contracts issued to citizens or residents of state..."); *In re Alexander*, 227 B.R. 658 (N.D. TX 1998) (holding structured settlement annuity paid to debtors following the death of their children in automobile accident was entitled to exemption as an annuity under Texas law).

strong financial oversight of life insurance companies by the state departments of insurance, structured settlements represent safe and secure investment vehicles for injury victims. As such, having a structured settlement as the cornerstone of your financial settlement plan can mean the difference between outliving the settlement or not.

Structured settlements and the complexities of settlement planning present many issues that require expert advice from a trained settlement planner. Carefully exploring these issues with an expert settlement planner is very important because the passage of time or receipt of cash settlement proceeds can adversely impact your ability to do such planning. Additionally, as you will read in subsequent chapters, considering public benefit preservation trusts as part of an overall settlement plan is particularly important for those who are disabled and receiving certain benefits.

Review Appendix A to learn more about the different types of structured settlement products available.

OPTION THREE: A SETTLEMENT TRUST

The third and final option for your settlement is creating a settlement trust to manage settlement proceeds. A settlement trust is often a good solution for protecting the monies you have recovered due to your injuries because of its inherent liquidity and flexibility. Settlement trusts can be used as alternatives to or in conjunction with structured settlements. They are typically irrevocable trusts (they cannot be changed) with spendthrift language (clauses limiting unnecessary or wasteful spending) that pay for all of the life needs of injury victims.

They are managed by professional trustees and can also contain special needs provisions that allow for the preservation of needs-based benefits. These trusts provide the liquidity that is lacking in structured settlements and offer greater flexibility while at the same time protecting the recovery. The investment options become limitless, and a trust can always be paired with a structured settlement. Having a professional trustee owing you a fiduciary duty (a duty to act solely in your best interest) provides you security and a trusted resource for life and financial management issues. Choosing the right trustee for your trust is critical, and professional advice should be sought to make the best possible choice. You do want to make sure that the trustee is experienced in working with injury victims and special settlement trusts since it is a different niche. Also, you want to make sure the trustee is properly licensed and has sufficient liability coverage as well as assets under management.

In certain cases, a settlement trust solution makes sense because of its ability to adapt to changing circumstances. When a disabled injury victim has needs that are not easily quantifiable or predictable—such as future medical needs due to complications or increased cost of care—the settlement trust can adjust to the victim's needs seamlessly. When a settlement trust is paired with certain fixed-income investment vehicles, such as structured settlements, you can enjoy the best of both worlds: guaranteed income for life that has sufficient liquidity and flexibility.

Settlement trusts have a variety of investment options. Several asset classes can be used to generate cash flows necessary for ongoing expenses and to grow the assets held in the trust with flexibility to adapt to changing needs. Typically, an annuity product, such as a structured settlement, provides a stream of periodic payments to the trust. In addition to an annuity product, usually a market-based reserve account is professionally managed but can be accessed when the need arises or circumstances change. This type of trust arrangement provides you with the guaranteed income you need, coupled with the flexibility and liquidity crucial for injury victims when unforeseen needs arise. It also provides enhanced creditor protection by combining different protection mechanisms with annuities and trusts.

Typical settlement trusts have provisions giving the trustee discretion to move money into other trusts if certain identified circumstances arise. For example, this is a common planning technique when someone is disabled and might need eligibility for government benefits in the future. The trustee moving money into other trusts could allow you to qualify for Medicaid/Supplemental Security Income (SSI) as well as preserve future Medicare eligibility by utilizing settlement planning tools such as special-needs provisions and Medicare Set-Aside (MSA) provisions. Until such time as eligibility is needed for public benefits, if ever, the trust can purchase private health care coverage and make use of the settlement monies without the restrictions that accompany special-needs trusts or Medicare Set-Asides.

A settlement trust can provide you with a combination of trustee services and asset management services, so you do not have to manage unwanted financial affairs. At the same time, your needs and wants can be addressed so that your focus can be on recovery. A settlement trust can help protect you from risks and provide you with a professional financial team to ensure your future lifetime needs are met.

WHAT I DID AT SETTLEMENT

As I said at the start of this chapter, the three options I outlined are not mutually exclusive, and injury victims frequently decide on a combination of options. That is precisely what I did when I settled my case. I broke my settlement into thirds, roughly. I took a third in upfront cash to pay for unreimbursed medical expenses as well as items I wanted to either purchase or pay off. I put a third into a structured settlement that made monthly payments to me for twenty years as an income supplement. Then I put the remaining third into a settlement trust to pay for future medical expenses I know I will incur at some point because of my injuries, but I don't know exactly when. That sort of plan is not all that unusual in most settlements, but it does somewhat depend on the circumstances of each particular settlement. That is why working with qualified experts who can help you make the right choices for your situation is vitally important.

Given what I know now, I wouldn't make any significant changes to what I did for myself. There are some newer structured settlement products that have become available that are indexed or market based that I might have explored. Also, I might have reconsidered doing only a period certain annuity for myself instead of setting up lifetime payments. However, I decided to opt for a higher payout of a period certain until I retired since I knew I could continue to work and hopefully put more money away for retirement through my work-related retirement plans.

CHAPTER 4

SETTLEMENT DECISIONS: GOVERNMENT HEALTH CARE—PROTECTING YOUR RIGHT TO MEDICAID AND SSI

Two primary public benefit programs are available to those who are injured and disabled. The first is the Medicaid program and its frequent companion benefit Supplemental Security Income (SSI), which are awarded based on disability and financial need. The second is the Medicare program and its frequent companion benefit Social Security Disability Income/Retirement (SSDI), which are considered entitlements and not impacted by income and assets. Both programs can be diminished or lost altogether when you receive a personal injury settlement, which can have disastrous consequences. There are also needs-based programs that help with food (food stamps), housing assistance, coverage for the military, and other specialized programs which are beyond the scope of this book. However, you should consult a qualified elder law attorney or other government benefit experts to learn about how the benefits you qualify for may be impacted by a personal injury settlement.

To illustrate the issues related to the major benefit programs, take the case of a laborer I'll call John Jackson, who was paralyzed when he was thirty. He did not have health insurance at the time of his accident, so the hospital applied for Medicaid on his behalf. Mr. Jackson qualified for Medicaid since he had no real assets and no longer had an income. His family applied for SSDI since he met the eligibility requirements. Mr. Jackson's lawyers settled his case for $1 million, which will help him pay for everything he now needs, but it is far less than what he needs to pay for all his future medical care. This is a fairly common situation and one easily solved with the right planning. To keep his Medicaid benefits, Mr. Jackson likely will need to set up a special needs trust. Since SSDI is not impacted by a settlement, those benefits are not at risk of being lost. If they had been SSI benefits, they would be at risk since they are needs-based, and a special needs trust would be needed to protect eligibility for them.

This chapter addresses the myriad of issues behind Medicaid and SSI and discusses how they can be untangled with the help of a settlement expert. You may also want to review Appendix B, as it has important additional information that coordinates with the information in this chapter.

MEDICAID AND SSI

Medicaid, which is funded by both the federal and state governments, provides basic health care coverage for those who cannot afford it. Eligibility requirements and services differ by state but include limitations on personal income and resources. SSI is a cash assistance program administered by the Social Security Administration that provides financial assistance to US citizens who are disabled, blind, or sixty-five years of age or older. In many states, one dollar of SSI benefits automatically grants coverage under Medicaid. Therefore, preserving some level of SSI benefits is necessary in most situations in case Medicaid coverage is needed in the future. Since you must meet certain financial eligibility requirements to receive Medicaid and SSI, the creation of a special needs trust might be necessary to keep these benefits in place at settlement. A special needs trust is one in which any assets held in the trust do not count as resources for purposes of qualifying for Medicaid or SSI, so injury victims who have received a settlement can continue to qualify for SSI and Medicaid.

SPECIAL NEEDS TRUSTS

Different methods for protecting needs-based benefit preservation must be explored for any disabled injury victim who is currently eligible. Special needs trusts allow injury victims to continue to access critical needs-based government benefits after settling their cases. Federal law authorizes and regulates the creation of special needs trusts, which require that you must be disabled.[9] Two primary types of trusts may be created to hold

9   To be considered disabled for purposes of creating a special needs trust, the beneficiary must meet the definition of disability for SSDI found at 42 U.S.C. § 1382c. 42 U.S.C. § 1382(c)(a)(3) states that "[A]n individual shall be considered to be disabled for purposes of this title…if he is unable to engage in any substantial gainful activity by reason of any medically determinable physical or mental impairment which can be expected to result in death or…last for a continuous period of not less than twelve months (or in the case of a child under the age of 18, if that individual has a medically determinable physical or mental impairment, which results in marked and severe functional limitations, and which can be expected to result in death or…last for a continuous period of not less than 12 months)."

a personal injury recovery, each with its own requirements and restrictions.

TYPE ONE: THE STANDALONE SPECIAL NEEDS TRUST

Standalone special needs trusts can be established only for those who are disabled and under age sixty-five. This trust is established with the personal injury victim's recovery, for the victim's own benefit. It can be established by the victim, a parent, a grandparent, or a guardian, or by court order.

TYPE TWO: THE POOLED SPECIAL NEEDS TRUST

A pooled trust can be established with a disabled injury victim's funds, regardless of age. Like a stand-alone trust, this trust is established with the personal injury victim's recovery, for the victim's own benefit, and can be established by the victim, a parent, a grandparent, or a guardian, or by court order.

Comparing and contrasting the two types of special needs trusts most commonly used with personal injury settlements is helpful. Pooled trusts and stand-alone trusts differ in several significant ways. Five primary differences are outlined in the following chart:

Stand-Alone Special Needs Trust	Pooled Special Needs Trust
Can only be created for those **under** the age of 65.	Can be created for someone of **any** age.
Individually drafted for someone who is disabled. Provisions are unique and tailored to the trust beneficiary. A qualified elder law attorney who understands the unique needs of a personal injury victim should be consulted to assist with drafting the stand-alone special needs trust.	Not individually drafted. A disabled individual joins an established master trust, and his or her funds are pooled for investment purposes with those of other beneficiaries. Beneficiaries have their own sub-accounts where an accounting of their funds is maintained. A qualified elder law attorney who understands the unique needs of a personal injury victim should be consulted to assist with joining a pooled trust.
Trustee may be an individual but is typically a bank or trust company who may or may not handle investment of the trust assets. Investments may be personalized for the trust beneficiary's circumstances.	Trustee is a nonprofit entity who oversees distributions but often delegates investment functions to a third-party money manager using model portfolios.
All funds left in trust at death must be used to repay Medicaid for services provided to the trust beneficiary.	All funds left in trust at death may be retained by the nonprofit instead of repaying Medicaid for services provided, allowing an injury victim to make a charitable donation to the nonprofit and avoid repayment to Medicaid.
No startup costs except the legal fee to draft the trust, which can vary greatly. Most trustees charge an ongoing annual fee, typically a percentage of the trust assets. These fees vary from 1% to 3%, depending on how much money is in the trust. A stand-alone special needs trust will offer unlimited investment choices for the funds held in the trust.	Typically have a one-time fee at inception, ranging from $500 to $2,000 (often much cheaper than the cost of establishing a stand-alone special needs trust). Most nonprofit trustees charge an ongoing annual fee, typically a percentage of the trust assets. These fees vary from 1% to 2%. A pooled special needs trust will offer fewer investment choices—oftentimes, only one choice.

One of the most important differences between a pooled trust and stand-alone is who acts as trustee. With a stand-alone special needs trust, a trustee must be selected, unlike the pooled trust, where the nonprofit entity named in the trust documents is automatically the trustee. Having a hand in the selection of the trust company or bank acting as trustee provides some peace of mind to the family or loved ones. However, it is important to have a trustee experienced in dealing with needs-based government benefit eligibility requirements so that only proper distributions are made. Many banks and trust companies do not want to administer special needs trusts with a trust balance under $1,000,000, which can make it difficult to find the right trustee. Most pooled special needs trusts will accept any amount of funding, and most nonprofit trustees are experienced in dealing with people receiving disability-based public benefits.

As outlined in a previous chapter, choosing the right trustee for your trust is critical, and professional advice should be sought to make the best possible choice. You do want to make sure that the trustee is experienced in working with injury victims and specifically special needs trusts since it is a different niche. Also, you want to make sure the trustee is properly licensed and has sufficient liability coverage as well as assets under management.

The major limitation of all types of special needs trusts is that the money held in the trust can be used only for the sole benefit of the person for whom the trust was created (the trust beneficiary). You, as the disabled injury victim, cannot withdraw money and gift it to a charity or give it to family, for example. The purpose of the special needs trust is to retain Medicaid eligibility and to use trust funds to meet the supplemental, or "special needs," of the beneficiary. These needs are defined quite broadly, however, and include things that improve health or comfort, such as non-Medicaid-covered medical and dental expenses, trained medical assistance staff, independent medical check-ups, medical equipment, supplies, cognitive and visual training programs, respiratory care and rehabilitation (physical, occupational, speech, visual, and cognitive), eye glasses, transportation (including vehicle purchase), vehicle maintenance, insurance, essential dietary needs, and private nurses or other qualified caretakers. Also included are non-medical items, such as electronic equipment, vacations, movies, trips, travel to visit relatives or friends, and other items or services that enhance the trust beneficiary's self-esteem, comfort, or situation. However, special needs trusts cannot pay for anything considered food or shelter, because those expenses are part of the SSI disability benefit payment. If trust assets are used for food and shelter expenses, SSI payments could be reduced or eliminated. This might not be problematic if you qualify for Medicaid without SSI eligibility; however, many states grant automatic Medicaid eligibility based upon SSI qualification, so you must be careful about eliminating the SSI benefit.

It is important to note that special needs trusts are permanent and cannot be undone. However, what they lack in flexibility is more than made up for in the ability to utilize the settlement proceeds while preserving critical health care coverage along with government cash assistance programs. Before going back to the case example of John Jackson, a brief explanation of another option to a special needs trust (SNT) is appropriate. This option is called an ABLE account, but it has limited applicability given its restrictions. These accounts are tax-advantaged savings accounts only for those who became disabled prior to age twenty-six. An ABLE account is frequently used in conjunction with a special needs trust as the limits of what can be put into these accounts are relatively low. A maximum of $16,000, as of 2022, can be put into an ABLE, and if someone receives SSI, the maximum that can go into the ABLE is $100,000.

Let's go back to the case of John Jackson, the laborer whose settlement was not enough to cover his needs. His situation could be dramatically improved by a stand-alone or pooled special needs trust, which would keep the Medicaid intact by holding the settlement proceeds in a non-countable trust.

A trust also can be enormously beneficial when you need extensive long-term care as a result of your accident. For example, take the case of Jane Robbin, a sixty-eight-year-old woman who has never worked outside the home. She was recently the victim of medical malpractice: she suffered a stroke, which had not been diagnosed in a timely manner, and now she is disabled and needs to be in an assisted living facility. She has a private insurance policy that she can no longer pay for, and she qualified for both Medicaid and SSI after the stroke. In addition, she gets a small amount of Social Security benefits as a result of her husband's death.

Mrs. Robbin's case was settled for the insurance policy limits of the doctor who missed the diagnosis, which is $250,000—not enough to care for Mrs. Robbin on a long-term basis. How will she qualify for nursing home care paid for by Medicaid given the small settlement? Can she keep her SSI intact? Will the death benefits cause an income problem? As Mrs. Robbin is over sixty-five, she cannot create a stand-alone special needs trust, so her only option is a pooled trust, which will protect both her Medicaid and SSI eligibility. The Social Security retirement benefit likely is not a problem since she already has Medicaid and SSI, but if she does have an income problem, a Miller Trust (described below) could be established to deal with the excess income.

With both Mr. Jackson's and Mrs. Robbin's cases, what could have been a situation that caused the victims and their families years of uncertainty and suffering was easily turned into a positive foundation for their recovery. This was accomplished by creating settlement plans that include trusts to preserve their need-based government benefits—something that can be crucial in many cases to maintaining needed medical coverage.

You should be aware of two other types of trusts sometimes used for specialized situations at settlement. The first such trust is commonly referred to as a Miller Trust. It is authorized by federal law and can be utilized if an elderly injury victim has too much income from Social Security or a pension to qualify for some Medicaid-based nursing home assistance programs. Lastly, there is a third-party special needs trust, which is established and funded by someone other than the personal injury victim (i.e., parent, grandparent, charity, GoFundMe, donations, etc.) for the benefit of the personal injury victim. Typically, these are used when a disabled victim's parents want to provide their own money to a child or when a fundraiser is held for the injury victim. The victim still must meet the definition of disability, but payback of Medicaid is not required by federal law at death, unlike the other special needs trusts.

Review Appendix B to learn more about preservation of Medicaid and SSI with special needs trusts.

Chapter 5

SETTLEMENT DECISIONS: GOVERNMENT HEALTH CARE—PROTECTING YOUR MEDICARE ELIGIBILITY

Why should you be concerned about future Medicare coverage issues when you settle? The following hypothetical situation illustrates some of the problems that can arise after settling your case if you are a Medicare beneficiary. A sixty-two-year-old bookkeeper and Medicare-eligible individual I'll call Joe Lane slipped at a store and sprained his left knee. Joe had some pre-existing arthritis in that same left knee, and his doctor advised him he would need a left knee replacement at some point in the future. The case was ultimately settled with the store's insurance company paying a small settlement to Mr. Lane, based upon the limited value of a left knee sprain. However, when that insurer reported Mr. Lane's settlement, it listed a broad insurance code related to left leg pain, even though it paid no settlement dollars toward anything other than the knee sprain. The broadness of this code could result in Medicare rejecting Mr. Lane's future knee replacement surgery, leaving him with no set-aside funds to pay for that care and no Medicare coverage either. Worse yet, the ability to negotiate a conditional payment made by Medicare might be complicated by including care that is unrelated or by reporting overly broad codes. This all would have been easily avoided had the insurer reported a very specific diagnosis code for the sprain of the left knee.

This chapter covers issues for those who are Medicare beneficiaries at the time of their settlements and will need injury-related care in the future. As a starting point, you should understand that at settlement, you have an opportunity to set up a Medicare Set-Aside (MSA) to protect future Medicare eligibility for injury-related care. The price of failing to address this issue is the potential loss of future Medicare coverage for injury-related care up to the amount of the settlement. According to Centers for Medicare & Medicaid Services (CMS), since Medicare is not supposed to pay for future medical expenses covered by a liability or workers' compensation settlement, judgment, or award, it *recommends* that injury victims set aside a sufficient amount of their personal injury settlements to cover future injury-related medical expenses covered by Medicare. CMS's "recommended" way to protect future Medicare benefit eligibility is establishment of an MSA to pay for injury-related care until exhaustion.[10]

---

10   Sally Stalcup, "May 25, 2011," handout, Centers for Medicare & Medicaid Services, https://irp-cdn. multiscreensite.com/78727cfb/files/uploaded/Stalcup-CMS-Handout%202011.pdf. See also Charlotte Benson to Consortium Administrator for Financial Management and Fee-for-Service Operations, memorandum, "Medicare Secondary Payer – Liability Insurance (Including Self-Insurance) Settlements, Judgments, Awards, or Other Payments and Future Medicals – INFORMATION," September 30, 2011, Centers for Medicare & Medicaid Services, https://www.cms.gov/files/document/future-medicals.pdf.

In the end, victims and their attorneys must determine if future medicals have been funded by the settlement and, if so, what should be done to protect future Medicare eligibility for injury-related care. Most often, you can figure it all out by consulting with competent Medicare experts who can help deal with these complicated issues. However, you must understand that if you do not address this issue, you risk having to pay out of your own pocket for injury-related care if Medicare denies you care in the future.

WHAT IS MEDICARE?

Medicare is a federal health insurance program that everyone is eligible for once they turn sixty-five, or two years after becoming disabled under Social Security's definition of disability.[11] Injury victims who meet Social Security's definition of disability and have paid enough money into the system can receive disability benefits, regardless of their financial situations.[12] The SSDI benefit program is funded by workers' contributions into FICA (social security) or self-employment taxes. Workers earn credits based on their work histories, and workers must have enough credits to get SSDI benefits should they become disabled. Medicaid can be used to supplement Medicare cov-

---

11   SSDI beneficiaries receive Part A Medicare benefits, which cover inpatient hospital services, home health, and hospice benefits. Part B benefits cover physician's charges, and SSDI beneficiaries may obtain coverage by paying a monthly premium. Part D provides coverage for most prescription drugs, but it is a complicated system with a large copay called the donut hole.

12   While most often we deal with someone who has a disability, Social Security Disability also provides death benefits. Additionally, a child who becomes disabled before age twenty-two and remains continuously disabled since age eighteen may receive disability benefits based on the work history of a disabled, deceased, or retired parent as long as the child is disabled and unmarried.

erage if the worker qualifies for both programs.[13] For example, Medicaid can pay for prescription drugs as well as Medicare copayments or deductibles.

WHAT IS THE MEDICARE SECONDARY PAYER ACT?

An injury victim who is a Medicare beneficiary at settlement triggers consideration of issues related to the Medicare Secondary Payer Act (MSP). The MSP is a series of laws enacted with the goal of reducing federal health care costs.[14] The MSP provides that if a primary payer exists (such as liability insurance from an accident), Medicare pays only for medical treatment relating to an injury to the extent that the primary payer does not pay.[15]

When dealing with the application of the MSP, two issues arise at settlement: (1) Medicare payments made prior to the date of settlement (conditional payments, or "liens," are explored in Chapter 8) and (2) future Medicare payments for covered services (Medicare Set-Asides are explored in greater detail in subsequent chapters). As mentioned earlier, since Medicare is not supposed to pay for future injury-related medical

---

13   This is commonly referred to as "dual eligibility." For those who are dual eligible, Medicaid will pay Medicare premiums, copayments, and deductibles within prescribed limits. There are two different programs. First is Qualified Medicare Beneficiaries (QMB). The QMB program pays for the recipient's Medicare premiums (Parts A and B), Medicare deductibles, and Medicare coinsurance within the prescribed limits. QMB recipients also automatically qualify for extra help with the Medicare Part D prescription drug plan costs. The income and asset caps are higher than the normal SSI/Medicaid qualification limits. Second is Special Low-Income Medicare Beneficiary (SLMB). The SLMB program pays for Medicare premiums for Part B Medicare benefits. SLMB recipients automatically qualify for extra help with Medicare Part D prescription drug plan costs. Again, the income and asset caps are higher than the normal SSI/Medicaid qualification limits.

14   The provisions of the MSP can be found at Section 1862(b) of the Social Security Act. 42 U.S.C. § 1395y(b) (6) (2007).

15   42 CFR § 411.20(2) Part 411, Subpart B, (2007).

expenses covered by a settlement, CMS recommends that you set aside enough to cover future medical expenses that are Medicare-covered.

In certain cases, a Medicare Set-Aside may be advisable to preserve future eligibility for Medicare coverage. An MSP allows you to preserve Medicare benefits by setting aside a portion of the settlement money in a segregated account to pay for future Medicare-covered health care. The funds in the set-aside can be used only for Medicare-covered expenses for your injury-related care. Once the set-aside account is exhausted, you receive full Medicare coverage without Medicare looking to your remaining settlement dollars to provide for any Medicare-covered health care that is injury-related. In certain workers' compensation cases, Medicare approves the amount to be set aside in writing and agrees to be responsible for all future expenses once the set-aside funds are depleted.

The following parts of this book are an overview of Medicare, Medicare Set-Asides, and the considerations for creating a set-aside when you settle your case. As a starting point, you should understand Medicare coverages.

MEDICARE PROGRAM OVERVIEW

The Medicare program is made up of different parts.[16] Part A and Part B are thought of as "traditional Medicare," which includes hospital insurance and medical insurance. Part A is the

---

16 SSDI beneficiaries receive Part A Medicare benefits which cover inpatient hospital services, home health, and hospice benefits. Part B benefits cover physician charges, and SSDI beneficiaries may obtain coverage by paying a monthly premium. Part D provides coverage for most prescription drugs, but it is a complicated system with a large copay called the donut hole.

hospital insurance, which covers inpatient care in hospitals and skilled nursing facilities. (It does not cover custodial or long-term care—only Medicaid does). Part B benefits cover physician visits, durable medical equipment, and hospital outpatient care. It also covers some of the services Part A does not cover, such as physical and occupational therapies as well as some home health care. Part D is prescription drug coverage, provided by private insurers that are approved by and funded by Medicare. Part C, Medicare Advantage Plans (MAOs), offers all of the coverages through Parts A, B, and D but through a private insurer approved by Medicare. It is an alternative to Parts A and B coverages and can be selected and purchased by a Medicare beneficiary from private insurance companies.

There is a connection between Medicare eligibility and SSDI. SSDI automatically makes you eligible, after a certain period of time, for Medicare coverage prior to normal retirement age (sixty-five). This is pertinent as many injury victims become Medicare-eligible by virtue of disability.

WHAT AN INJURY VICTIM SHOULD KNOW ABOUT THE MEDICARE SECONDARY PAYER ACT AND MANDATORY INSURER REPORTING

An injury victim who is a current Medicare beneficiary should understand the Medicare Secondary Payer Act and how to be protected from the ramifications of non-compliance. The passage of the Medicare, Medicaid, and SCHIP Extension Act has triggered heightened concerns of all parties about settlements involving Medicare beneficiaries. Part of this Act, Section 111, extends the government's ability to enforce the Medicare Secondary Payer Act. Section 111 requires a defendant liability insurer to determine whether a plaintiff is a Medicare beneficiary ("entitled") and, if so, to provide certain information to the Secretary of Health and Human Services when the claim is settled. This is called the Mandatory Insurer Requirement (MIR). These reporting requirements make it very easy for CMS to review settlements to determine whether Medicare's interests were adequately addressed by the settling parties and to potentially deny future Medicare-covered services related to the injuries suffered by the injury victim.

The requirement of reporting causes some very real and difficult problems for personal injury victims who are Medicare beneficiaries. The biggest problem is the required disclosure of International Classification of Disease (ICD) medical diagnosis codes that identify injury-related medical conditions. These ICD codes potentially can create a situation in which care is rejected by Medicare in the future. If your attorney is unaware of the conditions disclosed by the defendant/insurer through the reporting process, some serious problems can arise when you seek injury-related medical care from Medicare in the future.

WHAT TO KNOW IF YOU ARE INJURED AND WILL NEED MEDICARE COVERAGE IN THE FUTURE FOR YOUR INJURIES

For many years, personal injury cases were resolved without consideration of Medicare's secondary payer status, even though all forms of liability insurance have been primary to Medicare since 1980. At settlement, an injury victim would receive damages for future medical that was Medicare-covered. However, none of those settlement dollars would be used to pay for future Medicare-covered health needs. Instead, the burden was shifted from the primary payer (liability insurer or workers' compensation carrier) to Medicare. Injury victims routinely provided their Medicare card to health care providers for injury-related care.

These practices began to change in 2001 when set-asides were officially developed by CMS as an MSP-compliance tool for workers' compensation cases. The set-aside requirement was designed to prevent attempts "to shift liability for the cost of a work-related injury or illness to Medicare."[17] Set-asides ensure that Medicare does not pay for future medical care that is being compensated by a primary payer by way of a settlement or an award.

MEDICARE FUTURES—CONSIDERING MEDICARE'S INTERESTS

Today, there is a very real threat of Medicare denying future injury-related care after your personal injury case is resolved. This can be triggered easily by the insurer/defendant reporting injury-related ICD codes to Medicare, which happens automatically now with any gross settlement of $750 or greater. Once a denial of care is triggered, to appeal the denial, a Medicare beneficiary must go through four levels of internal Medicare appeals plus a federal district court before ever getting the denial addressed by a federal appeals court. Therefore, addressing these issues at settlement must be of primary concern, particularly in catastrophic injury cases where denial of care could be devastating to an injury victim's future quality of life.

Consider this scenario. You are a current Medicare beneficiary and a plaintiff in an auto accident case. As part of the workup

---

17   Parashar B. Patel, "July 23, 2001," handout. Centers for Medicare & Medicaid Services, https://www.cms.gov/Medicare/Coordination-of-Benefits-and-Recovery/Workers-Compensation-Medicare-Set-Aside-Arrangements/WCMSA-Memorandums/Downloads/July-23-2001-Memorandum.pdf.

of the case, your attorney determines you will need future medical care related to the injuries suffered in the accident. This could be determined by either a deposition of the treating physician or the creation of a life-care plan for litigation purposes. Ultimately, you settle your case. Since you are a Medicare beneficiary and the gross settlement proceeds are greater than $750, the defendant reports the settlement under the Mandatory Insurer Reporting Law. The defendant puts some language into the release about a Medicare Set-Aside being your responsibility and specifies that you cannot shift the burden to Medicare for future injury-related care. Everyone signs the release, and settlement dollars are paid. The file is closed and then forgotten. What happens, though, if that course of action triggers a denial of future care by Medicare?

Medicare's position, that injury victims cannot settle their cases and shift the burden to the Medicare Trust Fund for injury-related care, is not new. Medicare has stated this premise repeatedly. But the first time Medicare actually submitted a notice of denial was in 2018. A personal injury victim submitted a bill to Medicare for hospital outpatient clinic services under Part B of Medicare. The bill was denied based upon a notice, in which Medicare said, "You may have funds set aside from your settlement to pay for your future medical expenses and prescription drug treatment related to your injury(ies)." The denial was related to a 2014 personal injury settlement wherein the Medicare beneficiary was paid money as damages for future injury-related care. This continues to be an issue in a handful of settlements that we see every year.

HOW DO YOU AVOID A DENIAL OF CARE?

Unfortunately, there is no cookie-cutter answer for what to do about Medicare compliance at settlement for an injury victim who is a Medicare beneficiary. Analysis and careful consideration on a case-by-case basis is required. In some instances, there may be an argument that future medicals aren't funded at all by a settlement. In other cases, there might be an argument that a reduced amount of future medical expenses should be set aside to satisfy obligations under the Medicare Secondary Payer Act because the case settled for less than full value. There are too many possibilities to give a simple one-size-fits-all answer.

CONCLUSION

To summarize, Medicare beneficiaries who settle their cases and attempt to shift the burden to Medicare to pay for future injury-related care might be denied coverage by Medicare. Medicare interprets the Medicare Secondary Payer Act as requiring consideration of their "future interests." Failing to address this issue can result in a future denial of injury-related care by Medicare. For these reasons, if you are a Medicare beneficiary settling a personal injury case, your settlement planning team should include a Medicare expert.

WHAT IS A MEDICARE SET-ASIDE (MSA)?

To better understand Medicare Set-Asides, you should also review Appendix C while reading the following explanation. An MSA is a portion of settlement proceeds, called an "allocation," set aside in a segregated account that is used to pay for future Medicare-covered services and which must be exhausted prior to Medicare paying for any future care related to the injury.[18] It is similar to a health insurance deductible, where you self-pay until you have spent out of your own pocket an amount equal to the deductible. According to Medicare:

> The law requires that the Medicare Trust Fund be protected from payment for future services whether it is a workers' compensation or liability case. There is no distinction in the law. Set-aside is our method of choice and the agency feels it provides the best protection for the program and the Medicare beneficiary... Anytime a settlement, judgment or award provides funds for future medical services, it can reasonably be expected that those funds are available to pay for future services related to what was claimed and/ or released in the settlement, judgment, or award. Thus, Medicare should not be billed for future services until those funds are exhausted by payments to providers for services that would otherwise be covered by Medicare.[19]

The amount of the set-aside is determined on a case-by-case basis using the cost of future injury-related care calculated over normal remaining life expectancy. For workers' compensation cases that fit within the review thresholds established by CMS, the set-aside details are submitted to CMS for approval. There are no formal guidelines for submission of general personal injury settlements, and the CMS Regional Offices do not review liability (non-workers' compensation) submissions presently. This means for any type of case other than workers' compensa-

---

18   "Workers' Compensation Medicare Set Aside Arrangements," Centers for Medicare & Medicaid Services, last modified November 14, 2022, https://www.cms.gov/Medicare/Coordination-of-Benefits-and-Recovery/Workers-Compensation-Medicare-Set-Aside-Arrangements/WCMSA-Overview.html.

19   Sally Stalcup, "May 25, 2011," handout, Centers for Medicare & Medicaid Services, https://irp-cdn.multiscreensite.com/78727cfb/files/uploaded/Stalcup-CMS-Handout%202011.pdf.

tion, there is no CMS review and approval process; the honor system is used instead.

WHAT IF THERE ISN'T ENOUGH MONEY TO SET ASIDE? A REDUCTION METHOD

You might be wondering what happens if the amount of your settlement does not include enough money to set aside for all your future injury-related care. Unfortunately, there is no definitive answer to that question. However, there must be a framework to address settlements that do not make a plaintiff whole in the context of Medicare Set-Asides. Obviously, having one hundred percent of a settlement consumed by an MSA that you cannot touch, except to pay for future Medicare-covered services, does not work. So what calculation would determine the amount of reduction of a set-aside? One could take an "Ahlborn pro-rata reduction approach" (a US Supreme Court Case that dealt with Medicaid lien reduction). This approach necessitates an estimate of the total value of the claim, which is then compared to the actual recovery. From there, you determine the percentage of recovery that the settlement represents when compared to the total value of all damages. An Ahlborn analysis might look like the following:

$4,000,000 = Total Case Value (all damages)

$1,000,000 = Settlement

$400,000 = Fees (40%)

$600,000 = Net

$200,000 = Set-Aside

$30,000 = Reduced Set-Aside (Plaintiff recovered 15 percent of total damages)

There are no guarantees that CMS would approve this type of method to reduce an MSA. However, submission to CMS of a liability set-aside (and, for that matter, workers' compensation as well) is voluntary. Accordingly, if this method was utilized and the case was not submitted to CMS for review and approval, I believe CMS would be hard-pressed to argue that it was inappropriate. Given that CMS has ignored questions about how to deal with these issues for liability MSAs and has failed to provide any meaningful guidance whatsoever in this area, I believe one could make an estoppel type of argument if CMS ever claimed it was improper.

UNDERSTANDING THE RISK

If you decide that you do not want to set aside any of your settlement, then your attorney will likely document the education you received about the issue and ask you to sign an acknowledgement. If you elect to do a set-aside, your attorney will hire a company to do an analysis to help determine the proper course of action to protect Medicare eligibility. As a Medicare beneficiary, you must understand the risk of losing Medicare coverage should you decide to set aside nothing from your personal injury settlement for future Medicare-covered expenses related to the injury. Make sure you get the proper information on these matters to make an informed decision.

See Appendix C to learn more about MSAs.

MEDICARE COMPLIANCE CASE STUDIES

Consider a settlement for a forty-six-year-old man I'll call Jim Doe, who was injured in a motorcycle accident and lost both of his legs. He worked up until his accident, applied for SSDI after the accident, and was accepted in 2021. He became a Medicare beneficiary as a result of qualifying for SSDI. His lawyer is about to settle his case for $2,000,000 gross and wants to make sure to address Medicare-compliance issues. In this instance, doing a MSA analysis makes sense to document what is being done to deal with the MSP. The settlement will be reported to Medicare under the mandatory insurer reporting requirements, which could trigger a future denial of injury-related care. Ultimately, Mr. Doe must decide whether to set aside or not, but what was done and why should be documented for compliance purposes. This might be a situation where an argument could be made for a reduced set-aside amount based on reduction methodologies. In this example, the client likely would not be recovering his full value of future medical.

Secondly, consider the case of Jill Brown, who was injured as the result of a defective product. Mrs. Brown was thirty-eight at the time of her incident, a tire blowout in which she suffered a traumatic brain injury. She has applied for SSDI but has not been accepted yet and is not a current Medicare beneficiary. The defendant is insisting upon a set-aside and detailed language in the release. The settlement was for a "nuisance value" of $500,000. This is a case where definitively there is not an MSP-compliance issue. The client is not a Medicare beneficiary, and the settlement will not/cannot be reported to Medicare under the mandatory insurer reporting since there is no Medicare entitlement. Here, the plaintiff should reject the demands by the defendant to set up a set-aside and include Medicare language in the release. It is not appropriate, and she should not acknowledge an obligation that does not exist. If Mrs. Brown had been approved for SSDI, then arguably there could be an MSP-compliance issue, as she would have a reasonable expectation of Medicare entitlement within thirty months. This category of injury victims does cause some concern, but the settlement still cannot be reported to Medicare, so there is a very small chance of a denial of care.

Thirdly, consider the case of Bill Spencer, who was involved in a motor vehicle accident and suffered a neck and back injury. Mr. Spencer was fifty-two at the time of the accident. He was accepted by Social Security as disabled and has been receiving SSDI for the last twenty-three months. He will be Medicare-eligible by the time his case is settled for the $100,000 policy limits. He needs a significant back surgery in the future, which will involve a multi-level fusion. The future medical projection for damages is over $500,000, including that surgical procedure. During litigation, the defense took the position that the neck injuries were pre-existing and thus did not agree to pay anything for them. The defense's release stated those claims were being released but that they were for pre-existing injuries.

This situation is tough from the MSP-compliance standpoint, but it is a common scenario that parties face. Here, even though Mr. Spencer is not currently a Medicare beneficiary, he will be by the time the settlement is consummated, so the settlement will be reported to Medicare. Given the amount of expected future medical expenses and the fact that he will be Medicare-eligible when the case settles, MSP-compliance issues should be addressed. An argument very likely can be made that Mr. Spencer's future medical damages weren't funded at all because he has a $100,000 gross settlement and a future medical cost projection of over $500,000. Decisions in cases like these need to be properly documented, and the injury victim should understand the risk of setting aside nothing by taking the position that future medicals were not funded.

CHAPTER 6

SETTLEMENT DECISIONS: CONSIDERATIONS IF YOU ARE A RECIPIENT OF BOTH MEDICAID AND MEDICARE (DUAL ELIGIBLE)

In previous chapters, I have discussed the implications for settlement when an injury victim is covered by either Medicaid or Medicare. This chapter explores the planning you should consider if you are "dual eligible," meaning you qualify for both Medicaid and Medicare. In certain settlements, a Medicare Set-Aside/special needs trust may be necessary to preserve dual eligibility, which this chapter explains in detail. I explore exactly what dual eligibility is and how Medicaid coordinates with Medicare for those who are dual eligible. I also provide a detailed discussion of the techniques to preserve Medicaid and Medicare for those who have dual eligibility.

Consider a victim I'll call Mitch Smith, who was hit by a car while crossing a street in a pedestrian crosswalk. At the time of the accident, Mr. Smith was sixty-two years old and a low-wage earner but had paid enough into the Medicare system to be fully insured. When he was hit, he had very few assets. After the accident, he qualified for and started to receive SSDI and, consequently, Medicare. He also qualified for the Qualified Medicare Beneficiaries (QMB) Medicaid program. He received a settlement of $500,000, which was the policy's limit. Mr. Smith suffered primarily lower extremity orthopedic injuries and a slight traumatic brain injury. He anticipates possibly needing one future surgery to correct some of the damage done to his right knee. Because he is older and because of his injuries, he will never work again. He needs every penny of government assistance he gets. Medicare is his primary insurance, but Medicaid pays for what Medicare does not cover, so he has comprehensive coverage.

In this scenario, Mr. Smith faces a number of complex issues; he needs to worry about both a Medicare Set-Aside (MSA) and a special needs trust to preserve those precious benefits. Here, I recommend that an analysis be done to set up an MSA; however, that deals with only the Medicare preservation. For Medicaid planning purposes, Mr. Smith needs both a Medicare Set-Aside/special needs trust and a separate special needs trust to hold the remainder of the recovery. Holding the MSA inside a special needs trust prevents it from being a countable resource. This planning will make sure that Mr. Smith has the benefit of both Medicaid and Medicare coverage.

EXPLANATION OF DUAL ELIGIBILITY: THE INTERSECTION OF MEDICARE AND MEDICAID

Dual eligibility is not very common, but a subset of injury victims become dual eligible due to disabling accidents. By CMS's definition, dual eligible injury victims are those who qualify for Medicare Part A and/or Part B and also qualify for Medicaid programs. Medicare coverage can be obtained prior to age sixty-five if an injury victim qualifies for SSDI. It takes a total of thirty months for someone who is disabled to qualify for Medicare. (Medicare coverage begins twenty-four months after the first SSDI check is received, which takes five months and includes the month of receipt, adding another month.)

Medicaid coverage also is frequently obtained due to a disability. Some Medicare beneficiaries have such limited income or assets that they also qualify for state programs through Medicaid that pay for certain out-of-pocket expenses not covered by Medicare. Injury victims who qualify for Medicaid may be entitled to programs that help with expenses not covered by Medicare. In addition, some services that Medicare does not pay for can be covered by state Medicaid programs. For example, Medicare does not cover nursing home care beyond one hundred days, yet Medicaid does.

The programs that cover out-of-pocket expenses provide limited Medicaid benefits to those who qualify. Through these programs, Medicaid will pay Medicare premiums, copayments, and deductibles within prescribed limits. The two primary programs are Qualified Medicare Beneficiary (QMB) and Special Low-Income Medicare Beneficiary (SLMB). QMB is a program that pays for the recipient's Medicare premiums (Parts A and B), Medicare deductibles, and Medicare coinsurance within the prescribed limits. QMB recipients also automatically qualify for extra help with the Medicare Part D prescription drug plan costs. The income and asset caps are higher than the normal SSI/Medicaid qualification limits.[20] SLMB is a program that pays for Medicare premiums for Part B Medicare benefits. SLMB recipients also automatically qualify for extra help with Medicare Part D prescription drug plan costs. Again, the income and asset caps are higher than the normal SSI/Medicaid qualification limits.[21]

PRESERVATION OF PUBLIC BENEFITS FOR THOSE WHO ARE DUAL ELIGIBLE

Injury victims who are Medicare-eligible must carefully consider compliance with the MSP, as discussed in previous chapters. Injury victims receiving needs-based benefits such as SSI and Medicaid must plan to preserve those benefits, also as discussed in previous chapters. If you are dual eligible and you determine that a Medicare Set-Aside is appropriate, you then must consider the issues a set-aside raises with continued Medicaid eligibility. In many states, an MSA account is considered an available resource for purposes of needs-based benefits, such as SSI/Medicaid. Therefore, for someone with dual eligibility to maintain his or her Medicaid/SSI benefits, the MSA must be put inside a special needs trust, resulting in a hybrid trust that addresses both Medicaid and Medicare eligibility. This is a complicated but essential planning tool when you have dual eligibility.

---

20 Resources must be at or below twice the standard allowed under the SSI program and income at or below 100% of the federal poverty level.

21 Resources must be at or below twice the standard allowed under the SSI program and income exceeding the QMB level, but less than 120% of the federal poverty level.

CHAPTER 7

A SETTLEMENT PLANNING CASE EXAMPLE: PROTECTING THE RECOVERY BY PUTTING IT ALL TOGETHER

A victim I'll call Jan Black was in her early forties when she decided to have elective surgery on her back for degenerative disc disease. While she was being prepared for anesthesia, a problem developed during intubation, and the procedure was canceled. Mrs. Black was moved to the ICU, and no further neurologic monitoring was performed that evening. The next morning Mrs. Black was found to be irreversibly paralyzed. She then sued multiple defendants— including the hospital and the doctors—and eventually won a significant seven-figure recovery. Mrs. Black and her family had Medicaid coverage and SSI. She also had applied for SSDI. At the time of settlement, she was not eligible for Medicare since she had not been approved for SSDI and she wasn't sixty-five yet.

How does Mrs. Black protect her eligibility for public benefits in this situation? Is that the right thing to do? Should she consider private health care coverage? What about protection of the monies recovered on her behalf? Should she create a trust? What about structured settlements? Let's explore these questions further.

As a starting point, the first question is, does it make sense for Mrs. Black to give up her needs-based benefits completely by taking the settlement in a lump sum and becoming privately insured? This isn't a question that can be answered with a simple yes or no. She must consider multiple variables before deciding to forego coverage afforded by Medicaid and Medicare along with the needs-based Social Security benefit, SSI. First, will her private coverage be available for the long term? Or will her coverage, such as those available under the Affordable Care Act (ACA), be repealed at some point? Second, does she have needs that are not provided for by the private coverage, such as in-home skilled attendant care or long-term facility care? Given her injuries, Mrs. Black likely will need a significant amount of attendant care which isn't covered by private plans. These services can be very costly but may be covered by Medicaid in certain states. So, does that mean she should not try to obtain private coverage? Should she create a special needs trust to protect Medicaid and SSI? The answer lies in an analysis of the costs of the plans available privately and the amount of spendable income that results if a special needs trust is utilized.

According to a 2013 article by Kevin Urbatsch entitled "The Affordable Care and Settlement Planning," the numbers favor combining private ACA coverage with a special needs trust.[22] The following chart illustrates the financial benefits of combining a special needs trust with ACA coverage in California. (Numbers vary from state to state, and differences may be more or less important depending on local plan availability).

---

22 Kevin Urbatsch, "The Affordable Care Act and Settlement Planning," *Plaintiff Magazine*, December 2013, https://www.plaintiffmagazine.com/images/issues/2013/12-december/reprints/Urbatsch_The-Affordable-Care-Act-and-settlement-planning_Plaintiff-magazine.pdf.

PLANNING PROJECTIONS (40-YEAR-OLD FEMALE)[23]

Settlement Net Asset Level	$100K	$396K	$500K	$1 M	$2.868 M
Net Spendable Income – Annual Income [u][24]					
SNT Only [v][25]	$12,610	$23,751	$22,208	$33,484	**$67,500**
No SNT, Buy ACA Insurance [w][26]	EM[27]	EM	$11,196	$15,794	$67,504
SNT with ACA Supplemental [w]	EM	EM	$17,700	$20,684	$53,766
No SNT, Expanded Medi-Cal	$3,614	$14,291	NQ[28]	NQ	NQ
Income Percent of Federal Poverty Limit [x][29]	34.80 percent	138 percent [y][30]	174.06 percent	348.13 percent	600.70 percent
Average Annual ACA Premium (Net Subsidy) [z][31]	$0	$0	$4,508	$12,800	$15,552
Average Monthly ACA Premium (Net Subsidy)	$0	$0	$376	$1,067	$1,296

Source: Merrill Lynch Wealth Management Analysis through the Wealth Outlook Program, May 2013.

---

23   The following table is adapted from: Scott MacDonald, "Special Needs Trust Planning and the ACA," *Plaintiff Magazine*, December 2013, 2, https://www.plaintiffmagazine.com/images/issues/2013/12-december/reprints/Urbatsch_The-Affordable-Care-Act-and-settlement-planning_Plaintiff-magazine.pdf.

24   u: After-tax spendable income, net of premium or special needs trust expenses, assuming 2.5% COLA through actuarial life expectancy of the beneficiary).

25   v: Net Spendable Income for special needs trust options has been reduced by $3,000 expense to establish the special needs trust and 1% annual administrative expenses.

26   w: Net Spendable Income for ACA options has been reduced by average annual premium and maximum annual out-of-pocket expenses for the respective income level (based on percent of FPL).

27   EM: Qualifies for the Expanded Medi-Cal Program.

28   NQ: Not Qualified for Expanded Medi-Cal Program.

29   x: Assumes 4% annual taxable income based on the settlement net asset level.

30   y: Maximum annual income level to qualify for the Expanded Medi-Cal Program is 133% of the federal poverty limit ($15,282) plus 5% of any income disregard ($11,490 * .05% = $574.50) = $15,856 for 2013.

31   z: Average of highest premium rate for that income level across the 19 California regions. Amount shown is beneficiary's cost after federal subsidy.

As the chart demonstrates, utilizing private ACA coverage but also keeping Medicaid/SSI eligibility has some distinct financial advantages. While that is true, it also is true that a special needs trust, which would preserve Medicaid and SSI, places many restrictions on how settlement monies may be used. Accordingly, this decision should not be made strictly for financial reasons. A careful analysis of all the issues is necessary. In the case of Mrs. Black, other considerations outweighed the use of a special needs trust. She and her family did not want the restrictions that come with the special needs trust. Since monies were allocated to her spouse and their children, all the family's assets disqualified her for needs-based benefits.

Even though Mrs. Black was currently ineligible for needs-based benefits, that did not mean she could never become eligible again in the future. She might have a need for means-tested benefits such as Medicaid/SSI and could also become a Medicare beneficiary at some point; therefore, she had a trust created with provisions that would protect these benefits in the future. The trust has provisions that allow the trustee to move money into a "special needs sub-trust" and a "Medicare Set-Aside sub-trust" when needed at a future point in time. The set-aside sub-trust is contained within the special needs sub-trust so that in the event that she becomes dual eligible, the set-aside will not cause an eligibility problem for needs-based benefits.

For the sake of analysis, let's now assume that private health care coverage isn't an option for Mrs. Black or perhaps might not be around well into the future. What are the types of benefits she should be concerned about preserving, and what are the techniques used to preserve them?

PLANNING TECHNIQUES FOR KEEPING MRS. BLACK ELIGIBLE FOR GOVERNMENTAL BENEFITS

So how can Mrs. Black's current and potential future benefits be protected?

Since Mrs. Black receives Medicaid/SSI, as discussed in Chapter 5, a special needs trust can be created to hold the recovery and preserve public benefit eligibility since assets held within a special needs trust are not a countable resource for purposes of Medicaid or SSI eligibility.

Mrs. Black has applied for SSDI, which means, technically, according to Centers for Medicare & Medicaid Services (CMS) guidance, she has a "reasonable expectation of becoming a Medicare beneficiary within 30 months." An injury victim who is a current Medicare beneficiary or reasonably expected to become one within thirty months implicates the Medicare Secondary Payer Act, as discussed in Chapter 6. Under this federal law, Medicare isn't supposed to pay for future medical expenses covered by a liability or workers' compensation settlement, judgment, or award. CMS recommends that injury victims set aside enough to cover future medical expenses that are Medicare-covered. CMS's recommended way to protect an injury victim's future Medicare benefit eligibility is establishment of a Medicare Set-Aside (MSA) to pay for injury-related care until exhaustion.

In certain cases, an MSA may be advisable to preserve future eligibility for Medicare coverage. An MSA allows an injury victim to preserve Medicare benefits by setting aside a portion of the settlement money in a segregated account to pay for future Medicare-covered health care. The funds in the set-aside can be used only for Medicare-covered expenses for the disabled person's injury-related care. Once the set-aside account is exhausted, the injury victim gets full Medicare coverage without Medicare ever looking to their remaining settlement dollars to provide for any Medicare-covered health care.

If Mrs. Black needs an MSA now or in the future, continued Medicaid eligibility could become an issue. Because an MSA account is considered an available resource for purposes of needs-based benefits, such as SSI/Medicaid in many states, if Mrs. Black's set-aside account is not set up inside a special needs trust, she will lose Medicaid/SSI eligibility. To prevent this, she should put her set-aside inside a special needs trust—a hybrid trust that addresses both Medicaid and Medicare.

FINANCIAL SETTLEMENT PLANNING CONSIDERATIONS

We have discussed Mrs. Black's public benefit preservation issues above, but now let's consider the management of her significant recovery. Should part of it be in the form of a structured settlement? What about ongoing management of her financial affairs? Will she need help from a fiduciary, such as a corporate trustee? There are no right or wrong answers to these questions. Instead, options should be presented to Mrs. Black to consider so that she can make informed decisions.

As I discussed in Chapter 3, she has three options. The first option is to take all the personal injury recovery in a single lump sum. If this option is selected, the lump sum is not taxable, but once invested, the gains become taxable, and the receipt of the money will impact her ability to receive public assistance. But as discussed, a lump-sum recovery leaves Mrs. Black's recovery at risk for creditor claims, judgments, and wasting. As the personal injury victim, she has the burden of managing the money to provide for her future needs, be it lost wages or future medical. Needs-based public benefits would be a lost option if she were to take a lump sum.

Mrs. Black's second option is receiving periodic payments, known as a structured settlement.[32] A structured settlement's investment gains are never taxed, it offers spendthrift protection, and the money has enhanced protection against creditor claims as well as judgments.[33] Mrs. Black could avoid disqualification from public assistance if she were to use a structured settlement in conjunction with an appropriate public benefit preservation trust. However, a structured settlement alone will never protect Mrs. Black's needs-based public benefits.

And Mrs. Black's third option is a settlement trust. As I discussed, this can be used in conjunction with the other options. Settlement trusts are typically irrevocable and managed by a professional trustee, and they can contain special needs provisions to allow for preservation of needs-based benefits. These trusts provide liquidity and flexibility that a structured settlement cannot offer, while at the same time they protect the recovery. In certain cases, such as Mrs. Black's case, this solution makes a lot of sense because of its ability to adapt to changing circumstances. When a disabled injury victim has needs that are not easily quantifiable or predictable, the settlement trust

---

32 A structured settlement is a single premium fixed, indexed or variable annuity used to provide future periodic payments to personal physical injury victims.

33 See I.R.C. § 104(a)(2). See also Rev. Rul. 79-220 (1979) (holding recipient may exclude the full amount of the single premium annuity payments received as part of a personal injury settlement from gross income under section 104(a)(2) of the code).

can adjust to those needs seamlessly. When a settlement trust is paired with a structured settlement, an injury victim can enjoy the best of both worlds—guaranteed income for life plus sufficient liquidity along with enhanced creditor protection.

WHAT WAS DONE TO PROTECT MRS. BLACK IN THE REAL WORLD?

An expert settlement planner created a plan for Mrs. Black that included a settlement trust with two "buckets." One bucket is a structured settlement annuity that provides a tax-free fixed yield stream of periodic payments to the trust that the trustee can then use to provide Mrs. Black with income. The second bucket is a cash reserve that is professionally managed but can be accessed in the event that Mrs. Black's living situation or caretaker needs change or she has an unexpected medical need. This gives Mrs. Black the guaranteed income she needs, coupled with the flexibility and liquidity that is crucial for injury victims.

The settlement trust created has provisions that give the trustee discretion to move monies into one of the two buckets—called "sub-trusts" in legal terms. These sub-trusts allow Mrs. Black to qualify for Medicaid/SSI as well as preserve future Medicare eligibility by utilizing special needs provisions and set-aside provisions. Until such time as eligibility is needed for public benefits, Mrs. Black can purchase private health care coverage and make use of the settlement monies without the restrictions that accompany a special needs trust or set-aside. She is able to get back to life now, all because of detailed planning and creative solutions.

CHAPTER 8

POST-SETTLEMENT ISSUES: LIENS AGAINST A PERSONAL INJURY SETTLEMENT

WHAT THE HECK IS A LIEN?

When you suffer a personal injury, most of the time a health insurance program—often your own—will pay for your injury-related health care. However, when you are injured by a third party and need medical care, most health insurance plans have terms in their contracts that allow them to recover the medical expenses they paid out if you end up recovering money for your injuries from the at-fault party. That's right, once you have settled your case and are still dealing with all the challenges resulting from the accident, you likely will experience a new set of problems: your health insurance provider demanding that you reimburse it for the medical bills it paid on your behalf. These types of claims asserted against a settlement by health care providers are known as health care liens, reimbursement obligations, or subrogation. These terms have slightly different meanings but are often used interchangeably.[34]

I know how infuriating this can be. When I was hit by a car while cycling, I was covered by my company's health insurance plan. I was hospitalized for three weeks, and my hospital bills exceeded $350,000. My health insurer paid $188,000 to the hospital (based upon its billing rates with the hospital) and then asserted a health care lien against my settlement for that amount. Once my personal injury case was settled, I then had to negotiate with my health insurer to determine how much of my settlement money it would accept to repay the lien. My insurer wanted the whole lien amount ($188,000) paid back to them, but I wanted to pay them back as little as I possibly could. Every single dollar I could save on the lien repayment would go toward compensating me for my injuries. After several months of intense negotiation, my insurer agreed to accept a little over $64,000 as payment in full.

You might be asking yourself: What is a lien, and why does the health insurance plan have a claim against my settlement? Under the law, the third party that injured you is liable for your medical expenses. So, when your health insurance plan pays for injury-related care because of an accident caused by a third party, it has a right of recovery against any settlement proceeds you receive. The bottom line is that your health insurance plan anticipates that you will be reimbursing it from your settlement proceeds based upon the plan's contract with you, or under pre-

---

34 Some liens are based on an underlying debt; for example, when a treater generates a bill for care that isn't paid, which results in a lien. Other times a lien may be based on a right to reimbursement, which means the lienholder has no right to recovery unless there is a third-party recovery against the at-fault party. Subrogation is a totally different concept, as under subrogation, the health insurer has the right to go directly against the responsible third party, stepping into your shoes. The two types of subrogation are equitable and contractual.

vailing law on this issue. Alternatively, the hospital where you were treated may assert a lien for services related to the accident, either because you did not have insurance at the time of the accident or because the hospital refuses to bill your insurance.

Your lawyer's obligation is to determine if there were any payments made by your health insurance plan that entitle it to reimbursement. Your lawyer should obtain the written lien amounts from those plans and, ultimately, pay back those plans. And sadly, yes, you do really have to pay back those liens under the law. For example, in my personal injury case, the plan was an ERISA (Employee Retirement Income Security Act) plan that had a recovery provision in its Plan Documents that allowed the insurer to assert a lien against my settlement. Another common example is coverage under government health care policies such as Medicare and Medicaid. Medicare is always considered a "secondary payer" to any liability insurance available to pay for injury-related care. However, in an accident situation, while Medicare does pay for the injury-related care at the time of the accident, it does so conditioned upon repayment at the time of settlement. When Medicare pays for injury-related care, federal law requires Medicare to be reimbursed from the settlement.

There are many different types of health insurance plans, and their claims against your settlement are governed by numerous complex laws. While this notion is probably very frustrating to you, it is the unfortunate reality. Recovering money from personal injury settlements generates millions of dollars a year in revenue for the health insurance industry and the government.

Review Appendix D to learn more about the different lien types and the strength of their reimbursement claims.

LIEN RESOLUTION EXPERTS

Asserting claims for health insurance reimbursement even has its own industry of so-called "subrogation recovery vendors." Over the last twenty-five years, these recovery vendors have become massive corporations dedicated to taking money away from injury victims and giving it to health insurance companies. The growth of the recovery vendor industry has been fueled by its ability to take all or a portion of personal injury settlements received by injury victims through the lien resolution process.

Many times, the law firm representing you in your personal injury case will fight these lien holders and their recovery vendors to protect your recovery and make sure there is more money in your pocket at the end of the case. You should ask your legal team if, in fact, they will negotiate and resolve liens themselves or if they will work with a lien resolution specialist with expertise in fighting subrogation recovery vendors. When my personal injury case settled, my lawyers did not negotiate my lien (at my request). Being an expert in subrogation, I negotiated my own lien since I knew I likely could get a better end result for myself. Lien resolution experts are generally paid a percentage of what they save, which aligns them with your interests. Hiring such an expert often pays for itself because you will get to keep much more of your settlement money than you would have otherwise; lien resolution companies that work on behalf of the injured have the expertise, insider knowledge, and proven tactics to reduce liens beyond what most law firms can achieve.

See Appendix E to learn more about why personal injury attorneys frequently hire expert third-party lien resolution companies.

CONCLUSION

Taking the time to really think through what you want your life to look like post-settlement is so important. Without answering the difficult settlement questions and examining the issues I have written about throughout this book, the transition from litigation to life could be a painful one. Your long-term well-being can be greatly impacted by the decisions you make when you settle your case.

Issues that arise at the resolution of a personal injury case require detailed knowledge about a unique combination of laws. If your legal team does not include specialists who focus on these issues, even the most talented trial lawyers can easily miss critical details. The ability to find and determine potential solutions to problems that can arise at settlement is critical for a successful transition from litigation to life.

I know firsthand how difficult this process is. Experiencing your life being turned upside down by the injuries you suffered due to someone else's negligence is tough enough. Then you must go through the difficult process of a personal injury case. And finally, you have to deal with all of the issues discussed in this book. It might seem too daunting at times; it did to me as well. However, at the end of it all is something really good—knowing the well-credentialed team on your side has put together a comprehensive settlement plan that will protect you as much as possible. This type of safety and security will allow you to get on with your life.

APPENDIX A - TYPES OF STRUCTURED SETTLEMENT ANNUITIES

WHAT IS A STRUCTURED SETTLEMENT?

Structured settlements are an innovative method of compensating injury victims through the use of annuities. Encouraged by the U.S. Congress since 1982, a structured settlement is a voluntary agreement between the injury victim and the defendant for future periodic payments. With a structured settlement annuity, the injury victim doesn't receive compensation for his or her injuries in one lump sum. Rather, he or she receives a stream of tax-free payments tailored to meet future medical expenses and basic living needs.

There are three primary structured settlement annuity products utilized as part of a personal injury settlement. Each of these options has benefits and certain drawbacks. A summary of each option with its characteristics is below.

1. FIXED STRUCTURED SETTLEMENT ANNUITIES

A fixed annuity is one whose rate of return doesn't fluctuate with market performance. It is a guaranteed product in that the life insurance company promises to pay a certain amount to you in return for placing your settlement money with the life insurance company. The rates of return are going to be similar to bonds and other long-term debt instruments. It is a conservative investment but doesn't have any downside risk. This is the primary drawback: conservative returns. However, since the rate of return is fixed, it is a safe, stable, and secured investment dependent only on the financial stability of the selected life insurance company.

A licensed insurance/annuity expert should be consulted to understand this product and its advantages/disadvantages along with a suitability determination.

2. INDEXED STRUCTURED SETTLEMENT ANNUITIES

This option is identical to the fixed option immediately above as it is also an annuity, but these have an equity indexed rider which allows the payments to go up based upon market performance. Indexed annuities credit interest differently from the fixed alternative, which is set by contract. For indexed annuities, the interest is credited based upon a formula tied to a specific equities index (an example would be indexing tied to the S&P 500°). This option gives injury victims exposure to the upside of the market without the downside risk. Interest rate performance is tied to a certain index. Some products have payments that can increase to an annual maximum of 5 percent while others are not capped at all. If the index is flat or decreases, the payments remain the same with most products. This is called an annual ratchet up. This is a unique solution that gives more potential positive upside over the fixed alternative.

A licensed insurance/annuity expert should be consulted to understand this product and its advantages/disadvantages along with a suitability determination.

3. VARIABLE STRUCTURED SETTLEMENT ANNUITIES

While not currently an option, it has been available in the past and a new product is in development currently, so it is worth outlining the option. Variable annuities interest crediting is different from the fixed or indexed in that it is based on a basket of equity-based portfolios. A variable annuity has investment risk and as such isn't appropriate for everyone. With a variable annuity, the payments from the annuity will vary based upon certain factors, including the performance of the selected portfolios. In the case of an annuity that pays out monthly, this means that each month the payments can change in amount.

A licensed securities/insurance/annuity expert should be consulted to understand this product and its advantages/disadvantages along with a suitability determination.

APPENDIX B - PRESERVATION OF NEEDS-BASED PUBLIC BENEFITS FAQ

Compiled from various sources

INTRODUCTION

When injury victims receiving needs-based public assistance (SSI/Medicaid/food stamps/Section 8 housing) resolve personal injury cases, they must plan carefully to make sure they do not lose eligibility for these programs. Most needs-based programs have a very low income/asset threshold, meaning that even a small settlement can make personal injury victims ineligible. The following explains one commonly used planning technique to maintain eligibility post-settlement: special needs trusts. A settlement team of experts can provide guidance about the possible mechanisms to deal with eligibility for needs-based programs as well as work with a lawyer to devise and implement a proper plan at settlement.

WHAT IS A SPECIAL NEEDS TRUST?

The primary purpose of creating a special needs trust is to continue the monthly tax-free SSI or disability benefits and secure access to Medicaid. A special needs trust allows a personal injury victim to receive a personal injury settlement/award without disqualification from SSI or Medicaid. This is because federal law allows money to be placed into a special needs trust, where it is not a countable resource for purposes of qualifying for needs-based public assistance programs (see 42 U.S.C. 1396p). In order to create a special needs trust, the personal injury victim must meet the definition of disability contained in the Social Security Disability statute (see 42 U.S C. 1382c).

IS THERE MORE THAN ONE TYPE OF SPECIAL NEEDS TRUST?

Yes. There are several different types of special needs trusts. Which one is used depends on the circumstances of the settlement, age of the injury victim, and nature of the government benefits being received.

1. Stand-alone special needs trust (disabled under the age of sixty-five)

Under 42 U.S.C. 1396p(d)(4)(A), this trust is established with funds (typically a personal injury settlement/jury verdict) of the disabled person for the benefit of a disabled person who is under age sixty-five at the time that the special needs trust is drafted. After the death of the beneficiary, the law requires that any remaining funds are first used to repay any Medicaid lien due for benefits paid during the lifetime of the beneficiary. If any funds remain, they can be distributed to the heirs of the beneficiary according to the terms of the trust. This is called a payback provision. This type of trust can be created by the injury victim, a parent, grandparent, or guardian, or by court order.

2. Pooled special needs trust/pooled trust (disabled person of any age)

This trust is created pursuant to 42 U.S.C 1396p(d)(4)(C). A nonprofit trustee administers it, and people join the master trust. It is established with funds of the disabled person; however, this person can be of any age (even over sixty-five) at the time that the pooled special needs trust is drafted. Like a stand-alone special needs trust, a pooled trust must also contain a payback provision. A pooled trust frequently has a very low minimum trust balance requirement and is economical to utilize. Injury victims themselves can create this type of trust.

3. Qualified Income Trust/Miller Trust

This trust is created under 42 U.S.C. 1396p(d)(4)(B). It is used for Medicaid recipients who have too much income to otherwise qualify for Medicaid (used in long-term care/nursing home situations) but not enough income to pay for care without Medicaid.

4. Third-party special needs trust

This trust is established by someone else (parent, grandparent, etc.) for the benefit of a disabled person. A third-party special needs trust can provide for the disabled person's comfort and happiness during his or her lifetime. When establishing the trust, the grantor of the trust decides where any funds remaining in the trust will go when the disabled person passes away.

HOW DO I KNOW IF I NEED A SPECIAL NEEDS TRUST?

If you do not have enough money to pay for all your future medical care and support needs from your settlement, you are disabled, and you are currently eligible for SSI/Medicaid, then you should consider establishing a special needs trust. Again, you must be disabled by the definition according to the Social Security Disability statute to qualify for a special needs trust.

HOW CAN A SPECIAL NEEDS TRUST BE FUNDED WITH PERSONAL INJURY LAWSUIT PROCEEDS?

Special needs trusts can be funded in two ways: (1) All the settlement proceeds can be placed in the special needs trust immediately. In this scenario, interest earned on the investment of the money by the trustee is taxable. (2) Alternatively, part of the settlement proceeds can be used to seed the trust, with the remainder being used to purchase a structured settlement annuity that will make payments into the trust. In this scenario, interest earned on the structure is not taxed. However, once payments are made into the trust and invested by the trust, the interest earned by the trust is taxable.

WHAT ARE THE ADVANTAGES OF A SPECIAL NEEDS TRUST?

The personal injury victim has access to Medicaid rates and services and can still purchase medical services and equipment at regular rates whenever necessary.

The trust beneficiary continues to receive SSI or disability benefits adjusted upward for the cost of living each year. Over time, those benefits provide a significant amount of money.

A trust is an ideal vehicle to provide continuity of fiscal management over a long period of time, even without consideration of eligibility for SSI and Medicaid; there are no annual guardianship reports to file, and trust withdrawals can be made on a regular basis as well as an emergency basis without a court order.

WHAT ARE THE DISADVANTAGES OF A SPECIAL NEEDS TRUST?

The main disadvantage is that the personal injury victim, or the victim's family, cannot have unrestricted use of the money to spend in any way they see fit. However, with good planning and under the appropriate circumstances, the settlement proceeds can be used to substantially improve the lives of the disabled person and his or her family, provide for future security, protect access to Medicaid, and manage the money in an efficient and secure manner.

Another disadvantage is that upon the individual's death, the state receives all remaining amounts up to the amount of the public assistance paid on behalf of the individual. This payback provision must be included in a special needs trust. Family members of the victim (death beneficiaries) are paid only the amount remaining after Medicaid is reimbursed.

HOW DOES A SPECIAL NEEDS TRUST OPERATE?

For purposes of maintaining SSI and Medicaid, the beneficiary may not have direct control of the funds. Instead, a trustee is selected to hold the assets, and that trustee is usually a bank or trust company. The trustee must be directed to maximize the benefit of the trust where appropriate, paying for only those items for which the beneficiary is not otherwise eligible from government benefit programs, such as SSI, Medicaid, group homes, nursing homes, etc. The trust must be irrevocable. When the beneficiary needs something, a distribution request is made to the trustee, who disburses the monies to pay for necessary items/services, so long as they are for the sole benefit of the trust beneficiary and will not interfere with needs-based government assistance eligibility.

WHO CHOOSES THE TRUSTEE?

The personal injury victim or the victim's family selects the trustee or trustees. Settlement planning experts can share their experiences in other cases and suggest trustees, care managers, social workers, and others who can help. If the injury victim selects a corporate trustee to invest and manage the funds available, a settlement planner can help navigate the relationship with the trustee.

WHAT TYPES OF ITEMS OR SERVICES CAN THE SPECIAL NEEDS TRUST PAY FOR?

The purpose of the trust is to retain Medicaid and to use trust funds to meet the supplemental needs ("special needs") of the trust beneficiary. That purpose is considered to be quite broad, however, and includes special education, health, comfort, medical and dental expenses, trained medical assistance staff (24 hours or as needed), independent medical checkups, equipment, supplies, programs of cognitive and visual training, respiratory care and rehabilitation (physical, occupational, speech, visual, and cognitive), eyeglasses, transportation (including vehicle purchases), maintenance, insurance, essential dietary needs, and private nurses or other qualified caretakers.

Also included are non-medical items, such as radios, records or CD players, televisions, VCRs, computer equipment, vacations, movies, trips, travel to visit relatives or friends, summer or day camps, college or technical school tuition, and other monetary requirements to enhance the client's self-esteem, comfort, or situation. Generally, the trust can be used to pay expenses that are not food and shelter, which are part of the SSI benefit payment. "Shelter" expenses are broadly defined and, for example, would prevent payments by the trustee directly to the lawn maintenance service employed to cut the client's grass. In some cases, monthly mortgage payments can be made by the trust; however, the payments might reduce the client's SSI monthly check due to the application of the "presumed value reduction" rule.

Medicaid will cover some of these items. For example, if Medicaid pays for a specifically fitted $6,000 wheelchair once every five years, but an injury victim needs wheelchair modifications or a new wheelchair on a more frequent basis, then the special needs trust can pay the difference. As another example, if Medicaid does not pay for second opinions prior to surgery, the trust can.

Sometimes the trust beneficiary is covered under a parent's or spouse's employer's group health plan. Yet many of those plans restrict the number of respiratory therapy or psychological counseling visits allowed. If the private insurance does not pay, the trustee looks to Medicaid. If neither pays, the trust is available to pay those medical bills.

What happens if the personal injury victim no longer qualifies for Medicaid?

If a personal injury victim wins the lottery, marries into (relative) wealth, inherits other money, becomes employed, or loses SSI eligibility and Medicaid for any other reason, the trust will continue to be available to meet the victim's needs in the same manner as any other type of trust or guardianship funds. The limitations on expenditures in the SSI and Medicaid rules, however, will no longer be a factor in decisions about disbursements by the trustee.

WHAT HAPPENS TO THE MONEY REMAINING IN THE TRUST AFTER THE DEATH OF THE BENEFICIARY?

The law requires that any funds remaining in the special needs trust after the death of the beneficiary be paid first to the state Medicaid agency or agencies to repay any Medicaid liens. Remember, although you are properly qualified for Medicaid during your lifetime, Medicaid has the right to demand reimbursement from your estate for any funds they paid for your medical care during your lifetime. Therefore, only if funds remain in the trust after Medicaid has been repaid will those assets be distributed to your heirs (whomever you decide them to be).

With a pooled trust, any funds remaining in the special needs trust after the death of the beneficiary may be retained in the pooled trust if the amount that Medicaid is owed exceeds what is left in the trust. In that case, heirs would not be entitled to any remainder left in the trust since Medicaid would be entitled to all the funds left over at death.

IF I CREATE A SPECIAL NEEDS TRUST, AM I GUARANTEED TO ALWAYS QUALIFY FOR MEDICAID/SSI?

No. If you win the lottery next week, you will no longer be financially eligible for any needs-based (welfare) programs like SSI and Medicaid. The trust will still serve as an appropriate vehicle to manage your settlement proceeds without any restrictions on using the money.

Also, there is no guarantee that Congress will not amend the Medicaid statute, or that the Social Security Administration staff reviewing the client's trust and new financial situation will not make a mistake and attempt to disqualify the client. However, Congress' actions in 1992 and in August 1993 have shown movement toward expanding access to Medicaid benefits for disabled individuals. It appears that Congress is attempting to encourage other family members and the courts to financially plan for and use additional resources to meet disabled individuals' medical needs. Regarding children and SSI eligibility, Congress amended the Social Security Act in 1992 to expand SSI benefits for children and to allow children who were previously denied but subsequently became eligible and received large retroactive awards to put such awards in special needs trusts.

Similarly, the Social Security Administration (SSA) has issued new amendments to its internal procedure manuals in March 1994, clarifying that individuals may be the recipients of trusts and still retain SSI (and Medicaid). New "deeming regulations" issued in January 1995 also are more expansive and extend SSI and Medicaid benefits to families previously disqualified. SSA also has distributed informational brochures to clients, telling them that correctly drafted trusts will not eliminate eligibility for SSI benefits. However, literally tens of thousands of caseworkers across the country are making individual claims decisions every day. No one can guarantee that they will not make mistakes and deny claims for continued SSI and Medicaid benefits that should be approved.

One thing is absolutely guaranteed: if the settlement award is more than $2,000 and no special needs trust is created, you will lose SSI and Medicaid when the Social Security Administration is advised of the settlement award. Furthermore, it is a crime to fail to report such a settlement to Social Security if the settlement will affect future eligibility, and the Social Security Administration may seek to recover the resulting over-payments through collection by the US Attorney's office.

CONCLUSION

Anyone on asset-sensitive benefits who resolves a personal injury claim should consider the special needs trust options. Plaintiffs now can maximize their recovery even in cases with limited insurance coverage.

APPENDIX C - MEDICARE SET-ASIDE FAQ

Compiled from various sources

WHAT IS MEDICARE'S BASIS FOR SET-ASIDES?

"Section 1862(b)(2)(A)(ii) of the Social Security Act precludes Medicare payment for services to the extent that payment has been made or can reasonably be expected to be made promptly under liability insurance. This also governs workers' compensation. 42 CFR 411.50 defines liability insurance. Anytime a settlement, judgment, or award provides funds for future medical services, it can reasonably be expected that those funds are available to pay for Medicare-covered future services related to what was claimed and/or released in the settlement, judgment, or award. Thus, Medicare should not be billed for future services until those funds are exhausted by payments to providers for services that would otherwise be covered by Medicare."

—SALLY STALCUP, MSP REGIONAL COORDINATOR
FOR THE CENTERS FOR MEDICARE &
MEDICAID SERVICES, DALLAS, TEXAS

WHAT IS A MEDICARE SET-ASIDE?

A Medicare Set-Aside (MSA) is a tool that allows an injury victim to preserve Medicare benefits by setting aside a portion of the settlement money in a segregated account to pay for future Medicare-covered medical services. The funds in the set-aside can be used only for Medicare-covered expenses related to the personal injury settlement, award, or judgment. Once the set-aside account is exhausted, the injury victim receives full Medicare coverage without Medicare ever looking to remaining settlement dollars to provide for any Medicare-covered health care. Medicare may approve the amount to be set aside in writing and agree to be responsible for all future expenses once the set-aside funds are depleted. However, Medicare has no requirement to review and approve the set-aside amount. Many regional offices for Medicare refuse to review/approve set-asides, so it may be impossible to get written approval. If the settlement is a workers' compensation settlement, then the set-aside is reviewed and approved.

WHO POTENTIALLY NEEDS AN MSA, AND WHY DO YOU NEED ONE?

If you are currently a Medicare beneficiary and you settle your case, you may want to consider creating an MSA. In addition, if you are not a current Medicare beneficiary but have a "reasonable expectation" of Medicare enrollment within 30 months of the settlement date, then you may want to consider establishing an MSA. If you fall into one of these two categories, and you do not set up an MSA, then you could lose Medicare eligibility for your personal-injury-related medical conditions.

WHO DETERMINES THE AMOUNT SET ASIDE?

A professional who specializes in allocations examines your injury-related medical records and makes recommendations based on the amount of future care that will be covered by Medicare. The company hired to perform the allocation determines how much of your future medical care is covered by Medicare and then multiplies that by your remaining life expectancy to determine the suggested amount of the set-aside. Medicare does not necessarily simply accept the allocation recommendation; it could require more to be set aside than the amount suggested. However, outside of workers' compensation settlements, that is a rare occurrence.

HOW IS THE SET-ASIDE FUNDED?

The set-aside can be funded with a single lump sum out of the settlement proceeds or with future periodic payments using a structured settlement. A single-lump-sum funding makes the set-aside easier to administer but means more must be set aside than when using a periodic payment arrangement. Funding with future periodic payments via a structured settlement makes the administration of the set-aside more difficult, but it is a much cheaper way of funding the set-aside.

When a set-aside is funded with a lump sum, as soon as the account is exhausted, Medicare begins to pay for injury-related health care. However, when a set-aside is funded with periodic payments via a structured settlement annuity, it functions much like a yearly insurance deductible. Each year, the structured payment flows into the set-aside, and, when the funds are exhausted for that year, Medicare begins paying for services related to the physical injury. If the funds are not all spent in the year the periodic payment is made, they carry over to the next year. Thus, with structured settlement funding, Medicare pays only once all funds for any given year have been exhausted.

WHY IS A RATED AGE WITH A STRUCTURED SETTLEMENT SO IMPORTANT TO MY MSA?

Age ratings can save on the cost of the structured settlement annuity and reduce the amount of the set-aside. A rated age is a life-expectancy-adjusted age used to calculate the cost of a structured settlement. Receiving a rated age means that the life insurance company has decided that your life expectancy is less than normal due to your medical conditions and accordingly allows the annuity to be priced as if you were older. Shortened life expectancy translates into a lower structured settlement cost when compared to a structured settlement priced with normal life expectancy. Additionally, Centers for Medicare & Medicaid Services (CMS) considers a reduction in life expectancy when determining how much must be set aside. As evidence of reduction of life expectancy, CMS looks at the median age rating issued by the life insurance companies issuing age ratings. Therefore, not only does funding a set-aside with a structure cost less, but it also reduces how much must be set aside in the first place.

WHY SHOULD I FUND MY MSA WITH A STRUCTURED SETTLEMENT ANNUITY?

Purchasing a stream of benefits today that will provide benefits tomorrow provides a cost savings, especially when a rated age is involved. What this means is that less money must be set aside when a structure is used to fund the set-aside. In addition, interest earned on the funds in the structured settlement is not taxable. The structure becomes a tax-free, cost-free investment to fund the set-aside. CMS routinely approves set-asides being funded with structured settlement annuities and mentions their use in memorandums regarding MSAs.

WHAT DO I TELL MY HEALTH CARE PROVIDERS IF I HAVE AN MSA?

Before you get treatment for your accident-related injury, you must advise your health care providers about your MSA. Your health care providers should bill you directly, and you should pay them out of your MSA account, if:

- The treatment or prescription is for the accident-related injury, and
- The treatment or prescription is something Medicare covers.

IF I AM NOT YET ELIGIBLE FOR MEDICARE, CAN I USE THE MSA FUNDS?

For those who are not yet Medicare beneficiaries, the MSA may be used prior to becoming a beneficiary because the amount of the set-aside was based on the date of the expected settlement. Use of the MSA is limited to services that are related to the personal injury conditions and services that would be covered by Medicare if the injury victim were a Medicare beneficiary.

WILL THE MSA ALSO PROTECT MY MEDICAID ELIGIBILITY?

No. An MSA only protects future Medicare eligibility. If you receive Medicaid in addition to Medicare, a special needs trust might be necessary to preserve Medicaid eligibility. If necessary, a hybrid MSA/special needs trust can be created to deal with this issue.

IF I AM NO LONGER ENTITLED TO MEDICARE, CAN I WITHDRAW FUNDS FROM THE MSA?

No. You are not entitled to the release of the MSA funds if you lose your Medicare entitlement. However, the funds in the MSA may be expended for medical expenses specified in the MSA arrangement until Medicare entitlement is re-established or the MSA is exhausted.

WHAT HAPPENS TO THE FUNDS IN THE MSA WHEN I PASS AWAY?

The MSA funds, either in lump-sum or structured settlement (if guaranteed), go to your beneficiaries identified under the MSA arrangement. Medicare requires the funds to be used only for your future Medicare-covered, injury-related expenses. Therefore, once you pass away, those funds can flow to your family or named beneficiary. If a structured settlement is set up and you want money to go to your family or named beneficiary, you should request that the annuity be "guaranteed" instead of life only.

APPENDIX D - TYPES OF LIENS ASSERTED AGAINST A PERSONAL INJURY SETTLEMENT AND RESOLUTION

ERISA LIENS

The Employee Retirement Income Security Act (ERISA) was passed by Congress and signed into law by President Ford. According to the US Department of Labor, ERISA "protects the interests of employee benefit plan participants and their beneficiaries. It requires plan sponsors to provide plan information to participants. It establishes standards of conduct for plan managers and other fiduciaries. It also establishes enforcement provisions to ensure that plan funds are protected and that qualifying participants receive their benefits, even if a company goes bankrupt." Many lawyers and lien resolution experts do not agree with that statement when it comes to protecting plan participants as it relates to resolution of ERISA liens, but that is the stated purpose.

ERISA governs nearly all employer-based health plans. The primary exceptions are government employer plans governed by the Federal Employees Health Benefits Act (FEHBA) and state government or church plans governed by state law. Most, if not all, ERISA health insurance plans produce policies stating that injuries caused by a liable third party are not a covered expense and require reimbursement if a plan pays for injury-related medical expenses (often referred to as a subrogation clause). ERISA provides that health plans qualifying under its provisions can bring a civil action under section 502(a)(3) to obtain equitable relief to enforce the terms of the plan. Appropriate equitable relief is really the only enforcement mechanism an ERISA plan can utilize to address its reimbursement rights. That is to say, an ERISA plan can only enforce its rights against your settlement by asserting an "equitable" lien against an identifiable pot of money (your settlement). While, in theory, there is some distinction between rights at equity and those available through subrogation law and by contract, in practice, all this means is that they can still recover money from your settlement.

ERISA is a "compressive and reticulated statute," which means that the law on this subject is quite complicated. So, the US Supreme Court has clarified exactly what is appropriate equitable relief under ERISA over the last twenty years. Starting in 2006, the US Supreme Court began to clarify and articulate just how powerful a self-funded ERISA plan's recovery rights are under federal law. To sum it up, an ERISA plan's right of recovery is determined by whether the plan is "self-funded" or "insured." If a plan is insured, it is subject to state law and its rights of recovery are lessened based on the law of the state. However, if it is self-funded, then its recovery rights are likely very strong because the Supreme Court decisions have given these plans the ability to write whatever reimbursement terms they want into their policies. As those decisions indicate the vital importance of the plan language, reviewing plan documents is a critical first step in properly evaluating the strength of a reimbursement claim made by an ERISA plan. The ability to reduce an ERISA plan's lien ultimately rests on the strength of the plan language in terms of recovery rights by the ERISA plan.

MEDICAID LIENS

Those who are disabled and receive Medicaid benefits most likely will have Medicaid liens when their cases are settled. Every state must comply with federal Medicaid statutes and regulations to participate in the joint federal-state Medicaid program. Pursuant to federal law, the federal Medicaid program requires every participating state to enact a "third party liability" provision that empowers a state to seek reimbursement from liable third parties for injury-related medical expenditures paid on behalf of Medicaid recipients. In order to comply with this requirement, a state Medicaid program must have statutory provisions under which the Medicaid recipient is considered to have assigned to the state his or her right to recover the medical expenses paid by Medicaid from the liable third parties. That is to say, a state Medicaid agency must recover money from an injury victim who has had medical treatment paid for by Medicaid due to a personal injury claim.

Despite the mandate in federal law for state Medicaid agencies to seek reimbursement from liable third parties by way of "acquiring the rights of such individual to payment by any other party for such health care items or services," important limitations on a state's recovery rights protect the Medicaid recipient's property. The limitation comes from the federal anti-lien statute that proclaims "[n]o lien may be imposed against the property of any individual prior to his death on account of medical assistance paid," and the federal anti-recovery statute that states "[n]o adjustment or recovery of any medical assistance correctly paid on behalf of an individual under the State plan may be made."

The tension between these provisions in federal law and state law recovery statutes has become the source of litigation in both federal and state courts. When these cases reached the top court of the country, the US Supreme Court held that federal provisions preempt and limit a state's right to seek reimbursement from a Medicaid recipient's settlement to the extent that it reaches elements of damages beyond past medical expenses. Therefore, in most states, a reduction of the Medicaid lien can be accomplished by negotiating with the state Medicaid agency or its recovery contractor based upon arguments using Supreme Court precedent.

MEDICARE CONDITIONAL PAYMENTS

Congress has given the Centers for Medicare and Medicaid Services (CMS) both subrogation rights and the right to bring an independent cause of action to recover its conditional payment from "any or all entities that are or were required or responsible...to make payment with respect to the same item or service (or any portion thereof) under a primary plan." Most ominously, CMS may seek to recover double damages if it brings an independent cause of action. Given all of the foregoing, Medicare subrogation law is a problematic area for personal injury settlements and must be addressed.

The repayment formula for Medicare is set by the Code of Federal Regulations. If an attorney was required to obtain the settlement funds pursuant to these federal regulations, there is a built-in reduction for "procurement costs" (attorney fees and costs). However, the formula does not consider liability-related issues in the case, caps on damages, or policy limit issues. As a result, the entire settlement in certain cases must be used to reimburse Medicare. The only alternative is to appeal, which requires you to go through multiple levels of internal Medicare appeals and then federal court before potentially getting a reduction in the amount owed. What makes an appeal even more unattractive is that interest continues to accrue during the appeal so long as the Final Demand amount remains unpaid.

An alternative resolution method is to request a compromise or waiver post-payment of the Final Demand. By paying Medicare its Final Demand and requesting a compromise/waiver, the interest meter stops running. If Medicare grants a compromise or waiver, it issues a refund back to you as the Medicare beneficiary. You can request a compromise/waiver in three ways: (1) a financial hardship waiver, (2) a "best interest of the program" waiver, or (3) a waiver under the Federal Claims Collection Act. If any of these are successfully granted, Medicare will refund the amount that was paid via the Final Demand or a portion thereof, depending on whether it is a full waiver or just a compromise. These requests have a very high success rate and are thus generally worth your time and effort.

MEDICARE ADVANTAGE (PART C) LIENS

In the previous section, I addressed Medicare conditional payment resolution. Some injury victims, post-accident, will switch from traditional Medicare coverage to a Part C Medicare Advantage Plan. Therefore, even if your attorney has gone through the resolution process and addressed the Medicare-conditional-payment-related issues, he or she might not be finished. Lurking out there is the chance that a Part C Advantage Plan (MAO) has paid for some or all of your care. When settlement involves a Medicare beneficiary, all parties to the litigation must be vigilant and track down possible MAO liens or face the possibility of having to pay double the amount of the lien under federal legal precedents. Although shocking, this area of the law is developing rapidly in favor of ensuring reimbursement to MAO plans.

MAO plans use the Medicare Secondary Payer statute as the basis for their claims to reimbursement. Accordingly, their repayment formulas are the same as Medicare's, which requires only a procurement cost reduction. Typically, these plans are willing to negotiate and arguably must provide a mechanism for a compromise or waiver if they avail themselves of the Medicare Secondary Payer Act in terms of their recovery rights. The important thing is making sure these liens are identified and resolved because, if they are not handled, you could owe double the amount of the lien to the MAO.

FEHBA/MILITARY LIEN RESOLUTION

Federal workers obtain coverage through specialized plans provided under federal law. Military service members and their dependents are covered through different programs based upon their service. When injury victims covered by any of these government health plans are contemplating settlement, they must understand the recovery rights of their plans, which are summarized below.

FEHBA

The Federal Employees Health Benefits Act (FEHBA) program provides health insurance coverage to federal employees, retirees, and their survivors. Federal law governs these programs, which provide benefits to millions of federal workers and their dependents. FEHBA authorizes the Office of Personnel Management (OPM) to enter into contracts with private insurance carriers to administer FEHBA plans. OPM's contracts traditionally have required the private insurance carriers to pursue subrogation and reimbursement.

Unfortunately, federal law has empowered FEHBA plans to demand full reimbursement when a settlement occurs. Under the law, federal preemption very clearly applies, and state laws limiting a normal health plan's right of recovery have no impact on the arguments to reduce a FEHBA lien. Unfortunately, this likens FEHBA liens to ERISA plan liens in that they have very powerful recovery rights under federal law that preempt state law. Therefore, FEHBA liens can be difficult to reduce, depending on the strength of the recovery language in the plan's policy. As with most insurance plans, the first step in attempting to reduce the lien is reviewing the FEHBA plan's language that governs your health care coverage with the government. Some of these documents allow the FEHBA plan to have discretion as to whether they allow a reduction based on attorney fees or not being fully compensated for your injuries (made whole).

MILITARY LIENS

Three different types of coverage are available to those in the military and their dependents/survivors: (1) The Veterans Health Administration delivers health insurance to eligible and enrolled veterans, encompassing both inpatient and out-patient services at their facilities; (2) the Civilian Health and Medical Program of the Department of Veteran Affairs provides CHAMPVA health insurance for the spouse or child of a veteran with disabilities or a veteran who has died; and (3) the Department of Defense has the Tricare health care program for active-duty and retired service members and their families. When it comes to the military, the legal starting point for reimbursement claims is the Federal Medical Care Recovery Act (FMCRA). This law provides the federal government with the right to recover the medical expenses incurred for care of an injured beneficiary when there is a liable third party. Under this act, the United States government has a right to recover the reasonable value of the care and treatment from the person(s) responsible for the injury. Accordingly, health insurance coverage under the Veterans Administration (VA), CHAMPVA, and Tricare all have recovery rights under FMCRA and other provisions of federal law.

The VA recovery rights allow it to pursue recovery for treatment it has rendered that is connected to a compensable third-party claim. Under federal law, the VA has both an independent right of recovery from responsible third parties and a right of subrogation, assignment, and ability to intervene or join a beneficiary's claim. Unfortunately, resolving reimbursement claims for care received at a military or VA facility can involve significant delays because first you must request that a bill be generated. If you want to request a compromise or waiver of a VA subrogation claim, you must provide the amount of settlement, attorney's fees and costs, other medical claims and reductions, and overall policy limits available.

Tricare is similar to the VA as its recovery rights are governed by the same federal law provisions. And, like the VA, Tricare also has both a right of subrogation and an independent right of recovery from responsible third parties. Federal regulations do allow Tricare to include the expected cost of future medical related to the personal injury claim as part of its recovery claim. Tricare claims are generally resolved through the JAG office (the military's lawyer organization) where the military service member is posted. Reductions may be granted when there is an undue burden placed upon the injured party.

APPENDIX E - WHY LIEN RESOLUTION IS OUTSOURCED TO EXPERTS

Compiled from multiple sources

If applicable, Medicare, Medicaid, the Veterans Administration, and some other federal and state governmental agencies/programs, along with ERISA and private health care plans, will assert a lien on your personal injury proceeds upon recovery, based upon their subrogation rights. Most health care benefit plans (government or private) have provisions requiring that they are reimbursed for claims they have paid when there is another party responsible for your injuries. This is called subrogation. Pursuant to subrogation, you may be contractually or legally obligated to repay the government, your health insurer, hospital, service provider, and/or doctor for claims related to your personal injury case. Resolution of any applicable liens on your behalf may necessitate all parties to enter into a negotiated settlement with the government, your health insurer, hospital, service provider, and/or doctor for health care claims related to your case.

Due to developments in subrogation (lien) law, resolution of these liens has become complex and time-consuming, often delaying disbursement of a client's net proceeds. Your lawyer might ask permission to take the necessary steps to resolve all applicable health care liens, including hiring outside providers who specialize in resolution of health care liens. This could include retaining the services of a lien resolution group to resolve any liens present as a result of your personal injury recovery. These types of lien resolution firms specialize in resolving difficult health care liens on behalf of those injured. A lien resolution company's mission is to convince lien holders to accept the lowest possible amount to resolve their claims against your settlement.

Generally, lien resolution services can achieve the best outcome for personal injury victims. This is because of the complex nature of negotiating with government and private providers, as discussed above. Many lien resolution services' fees come from the savings achieved from negotiating the lowest dollar amount possible for lien resolution.

APPENDIX F - FREQUENTLY USED ACRONYMS

ABLE: Achieving a Better Life Experience or ABLE account

ACA: Affordable Care Act

CMS: Centers for Medicare & Medicaid Services

ERISA: Employee Retirement Income Security Act

FEHBA: Federal Employees Health Benefits Act

FMCRA: Federal Medical Care Recovery Act

ICD: International Classification of Disease

MAO: Medicare Advantage Plan

MIR: Mandatory Insurer Requirement

MSA: Medicare Set-Aside

MSP: Medicare Secondary Payer

QMB: Qualified Medicare Beneficiaries

SLMB: Special Low-Income Medicare Beneficiary

SNT: Special Needs Trust

SSA: Social Security Administration

SSDI: Social Security Disability Income

SSI: Supplemental Security Income

UM/UIM: Underinsured Motorist Coverage

VA: Veterans Administration

ACKNOWLEDGMENTS

Condensing my twenty-plus years of industry experience and my experiences from my own personal injury case into a book has not been an easy task. However, it has been a rewarding experience that has allowed me to reconnect once again with my passion for helping injury victims make that transition from litigation to life!

Without the love and support from my peers and team at Synergy Settlement Services, this book would never have been possible. My experiences working with everyone in the company, the injury victim clients we serve, and our talented trial lawyer clients have given me the inspiration to write my second book. I especially thank my peers at Synergy Settlement Services who helped with reading and editing content—Dan Alvarez, Anthony Prieto, Teresa Kenyon, Evelynn Passino, and Rasa Fumagalli.

Lastly, and probably most importantly, I thank my family members who did a lot of heavy lifting to help me edit this book. Thank you to my mother, Etta Lazarus, and Lindsay Tremblay for your help and support.

ABOUT THE AUTHOR

JASON D. LAZARUS is the Founder and Chief Executive Officer of Synergy Settlement Services, which offers health care lien resolution, Medicare secondary payer compliance services, and complex settlement consulting services. He is also the managing partner and founder of the Special Needs Law Firm, a Florida law firm that provides legal services related to public benefit preservation, liens, and Medicare Secondary Payer compliance.

Prior to joining the Synergy team, Mr. Lazarus was the President of a national settlement planning firm. Before that, he spent ten years assisting injury victims as a settlement planner. Prior to starting his settlement planning practice, he practiced as a medical malpractice and workers' compensation attorney in Orlando, Florida.

Mr. Lazarus received his BA from the University of Central Florida and his J.D. with high honors from Florida State University. He received his LL.M. in Elder Law with Distinction from Stetson University College of Law. He is also a Medicare

Set-Aside Consultant certified by the International Commission on Health Care Certification.

Mr. Lazarus' written work has been published by AAJ's *Trial Magazine, Florida Justice Association Journal, The Florida Bar Journal, NAELA Journal, Elder Law Report, Exceptional Parent, The Employee Advocate, News and 440 Report,* and *The Journal of Transnational Law & Policy.* His first book, *The Art of Settlement,* is a guide for trial lawyers and was an Amazon best seller.

He has presented on relevant topics for the American Association for Justice, Southern Trial Lawyers Association, Florida Justice Association, Florida Conference of Circuit Judges, Florida Workers Advocates, Workers' Compensation Section of the Florida Bar, Mass Torts Made Perfect, Lorman Educational Seminars, and countless local trial lawyer groups.

His written work has been cited as authoritative on Medicare compliance by the Florida Supreme Court in the landmark Joerg v. State Farm collateral source opinion and by the United States Southern District Court. He also has been a consulting expert and a testifying expert on the issue of collateral sources in many cases.

Mr. Lazarus is a member of the Florida Bar, Florida Justice Association, American Association for Justice, National Academy of Elder Law Attorneys, Academy of Special Needs Planners, Society of Settlement Planners (Past President), and the National Alliance of Medicare Set-Aside Professionals.